The Two Shall BECOME ONE

JIM HENRY
with MARILYN JEFFCOAT

The Two Shall BECOME ONE

A Wedding Manual

JIM HENRY
with MARILYN JEFFCOAT

BROADMAN
&HOLMAN
PUBLISHERS

Nashville, Tennessee

© 2000
by Jim Henry and Marilyn Jeffcoat
All rights reserved
Printed in the United States of America

0-8054-2290-0

Published by Broadman & Holman Publishers, Nashville, Tennessee

Dewey Decimal Classification: 265
Subject Heading: MARRIAGE

Unless otherwise noted, Scripture quotations are from the Holy Bible,
New International Version, © copyright 1973, 1978, 1984. Passages marked Living
Bible, The Living Bible, copyright © Tyndale House Publishers, Wheaton, Ill., 1971,
used by permission. NKJV, New King James Version, copyright © 1979, 1980, 1982,
Thomas Nelson, Inc., Publishers. NRSV, New Revised Standard Version of the Bible,
copyright © 1989 by the Division of Christian Education of the National Council of
Churches of Christ in the United States of America, used by permission, all rights
reserved. Phillips, reprinted with permission of Macmillan Publishing Co., Inc. from
J. B. Phillips: The New Testament in Modern English, revised edition, © J. B. Phillips
1958, 1960, 1972. RSV, Revised Standard Version of the Bible, copyrighted 1946, 1952,
© 1971, 1973. TMNT are from The Message: New Testament by Eugene Peterson
(Colorado Springs, CO: NavPress, 1993).

Library of Congress Cataloging-in-Publication Data

Henry, Jim, 1937–
    The two shall become one : a wedding manual / Jim Henry with
Marilyn Jeffcoat.
    p. cm.
    ISBN 0–8054–2290–0
    1. Marriage service—Handbooks, manuals, etc. 2. Weddings—Handbooks,
manuals, etc. I. Jeffcoat, Marilyn. II. Title.
BV199.M3 H465 2000
265'.8'42--dc21

                                                99-051953

1 2 3 4 5 04 03 02 01 00

CIP

Dedication

———— ❧ ————

S he has stood by me and journeyed with me, held hands with me and loved with me, prayed with me and interceded for me, laughed with me and cried with me, parented with me and grand-parented with me, witnessed with me and ministered with me, agreed with me and disagreed with me, worshiped with me and sought God's will with me. She has given forty years of her life with the focused purpose of becoming one with me in the indivisible union of Christian marriage—a union that will only be broken by death and that will be transformed into an eternal union with Jesus Christ, our Lord. It is with profound gratitude and unrivaled joy that I dedicate this book to my cherished bride, my beloved wife, Jeanette Sue Henry.

Contents

———— ✂ ————

Part 3: Appendices

Acknowledgments

According to *A Modern Guide to Synonyms*, "to acknowledge" means "to openly accept, though with some reluctance, the truth or evidence of a fact."[1] I am here to admit, confess, and openly acknowledge *without* reluctance the truth of a fact: this book would not be possible without the assistance of some talented individuals.

Thank you to Marilyn Jeffcoat, colaborer in this effort, whose expertise and enthusiasm for such labor is unbounded; Sandi Mathis, my executive assistant, who has unselfishly helped with this project in a hundred ways; J. B. Collingsworth, a pastor at First Baptist, Orlando, who contributed one of the ceremonies, and with his wife, Shugie, and assistant, Marty Wassman, have shared insights from their preparation for marriage classes which have helped many hundreds; Teresa McFadden, pianist at First Baptist, Orlando; Ken Varner, organist at First Baptist, Orlando; and Paul Skoko, Duncan Memorial United Methodist Church organist, who prepared the excellent wedding music appendix; fellow minister, Wes Thrush, who graciously granted us permission to use his vows for children; Jason and Jennifer Dukes, whom I married and of whose original ceremony I have included portions; the staff of First Baptist, Orlando, who helped prepare and revise our church's wedding handbook over the years; the praying and encouraging saints of First Baptist Church, Orlando, who prayed for me as I wrote, and who have demonstrated Jesus' love in so many ways that I often thank God that in his providence, he allows me to be their pastor; and all those whom I have had the privilege to pronounce "husband and wife" and who have faithfully kept their vows.

PART 1

Wedding Plans

———— ❧ ————

Your Wedding: Celebration or Commotion?

———— ❧ ————

While recently vacationing, my wife decided it would be a good idea to visit an exciting destination: the local mall! Wanting her to enjoy herself on our holiday, I escorted her to her vacation paradise. While my wife blitzed the stores, I did my usual male thing of taking my position in the food court, reading the newspaper, and doing some pedestrian sightseeing. Soon after I was seated, two women—one, apparently the mother of the bride, and the other, seemingly her close friend—sat down at the table behind me. Immediately, they began to talk about her daughter's wedding which had taken place the weekend prior to this conversation.

The mother of the bride talked about how nerve-wracking the experience had been for her and the family. She reeled off a litany of ulcer-inducing experiences: the wedding coordinator had forgotten something of major importance; the rehearsal had been a fiasco; the flowers were all wrong; the photographer was inept; the bridesmaids' entrance was a disaster; the bride's dress had not been properly altered;

and, to top it off, the reception had been a disappointment! As this frazzled woman sang the last note of "The Wedding Bell Blues," her tune diminished into a sustained sigh of relief that had a survivor-of-the-Titanic ring to it.

Her rendition of "The Wedding Bell Blues" reinforced my commitment to begin writing a new wedding manual. I soon began working on a new marriage manual that I prayed would help not only ministers performing weddings but also brides and grooms, wedding coordinators, wedding musicians, marriage preparation class leaders, churches seeking to establish wedding policies, and others involved with weddings. What resulted is not a warmed-over version of my first wedding book, although it started out somewhat that way. The more I worked on it, the more I realized this book must cover much ground not previously covered, and the more this writing project became an exciting, fresh new work to me.

In the time between my writing *The Pastor's Wedding Manual* and starting this book, I had had fifteen additional years of ministerial experience, officiated in scores of weddings, and seen monumental cultural shifts in society's approach to marriage and weddings. During that intervening decade-and-a-half, I had also seen tremendous changes in the perspectives of the wedding parties with whom I worked. Brides, grooms, and their families were no longer approaching weddings in the same way. All of these factors demanded that I readdress wedding preparation and rewrite wedding ceremonies.

The material contained in this volume has been tried and tested in the classroom of practicality. Over the last fifteen years, musicians, wedding coordinators, fellow ministers, brides and grooms, and their families have provided a wealth of information, ideas, and inspiration that I have tried to convey in this manual. Every effort has been made to arrange this material and to present ceremonies in a user-friendly format.

I believe this book will be a rich resource that will allow all those involved in wedding planning to know this is not a humdrum, been-there-done-that approach to weddings. These ceremonies and the careful details of planning for that monumental event can be so powerful and spiritually refreshing that onlookers and participants will know they have experienced a unique and distinctively Christian event. I believe its use will help those involved with weddings achieve the most meaningful celebration of Christian marriage possible.

After forty years of standing before God, couples, and witnesses to officiate weddings, my stance on the sacredness of a Christian wedding ceremony has not changed. God places a high value on Christian marriage, and we should do nothing to lessen what he has underscored. While my position has not changed, I have, however, observed some changes in the way Christian couples approach weddings today:

- Couples today seem more determined to have meaningful wedding ceremonies. More and more are preparing their own ceremonies and writing their own vows than in prior years. More time and effort are given in the wedding service preparation.

- More and more couples want their wedding to bear witness of their committed faith in Jesus Christ. They are unashamed of their desire that family and friends should know of their commitment to Christ and of wanting them to know Jesus as their Lord and Savior as well.

- More and more couples unhesitatingly accept our church's policy of participating in premarital counseling or preparation for marriage classes. Very few refuse to accept our standards for counsel, interviews, and preparation. In fact, they appreciate it and are quick to say so.

- More and more couples, family, and friends are coming to faith in Jesus Christ or renewing their Christian commitment as a result of being a part of a distinctively Christian wedding. By elevating marriage, the church bears a powerful witness to the community and the culture of the importance of the timeless institution of marriage.

• More and more couples are very serious about having a marriage that lasts. I don't know the numbers, but my best estimate is that of the hundreds of couples whom I have married, the number of divorces would be less than a dozen. It is not because I have some special glue that holds them firm to their commitment and their vows. I believe it can be attributed to the whole process of marriage preparation and the high view of the sanctity of the marriage ceremony itself. These couples have been surrounded with every effort to help the two become one for a lifetime.

I pray this book will be a helpful tool in your hands in whatever part you may play in the second most important event in your life (the first being your receiving Jesus Christ as Savior and Lord). I pray that God will bless you with all joy as you drink deeply from the springs of committed love in Christ.

CHAPTER ONE

Guidelines for Planning Church Weddings

———— ✤ ————

The church can help protect the sanctity of Christian marriage, as well as the wedding ceremony itself, by preparing a booklet of wedding guidelines for couples seeking to be married in the church. These beneficial guidelines should be prepared by the senior pastor, any other staff or lay member in charge of marriage preparation classes, the senior wedding coordinator, the minister of music, the church organist, someone representative of facility coordination, and other staff or lay members who might be regularly involved with church weddings (e.g., someone from food services or finance). The group should prayerfully put in writing the policies of the church regarding marriage by one of its ministers and marriage in the church. This manual should be adopted officially by the church in its customary procedure.

Using Wedding Guidelines

The wedding booklet should contain an outline of wedding guidelines that succinctly state the church's wedding policies (see appendix

A). It should also include information on scheduling a wedding and on working with the minister, wedding coordinator, and church musicians. The wedding booklet can also help guide the couple by providing information on selecting appropriate wedding music and wedding decorations. Included also should be a statement of the church's policy on photography or filming during the wedding ceremony. The booklet, likewise, should contain information on church facilities, wedding fee schedules and honorariums, church wedding receptions, and other miscellaneous wedding items.

The wedding handbook should be attractively prepared and positive in its approach. It should include a statement concerning Christian marriage, the sacredness of the wedding ceremony, and the privilege of being married in the Lord's house. The handbook should extend to the readers encouragement and a warm invitation to meet with the church staff to secure premarital counseling and guidance with wedding plans.

Scheduling the Wedding

Weddings held in churches usually have to be scheduled some time in advance in order to avoid conflicts on the church calendar and with the desired minister's schedule. Scheduling is also needed to allow time for premarital counseling and for wedding planning. It is advisable to plan at least four months or more in advance. Because of special events held at our church, some dates are not available for weddings. In addition to these dates, no weddings are scheduled on Sundays, holidays, or after six o'clock on Saturday evenings. In case of any conflict concerning dates, church members receive priority over nonmembers. Nonmembers cannot calendar their weddings prior to four months before the wedding date (see appendix A).

CHAPTER TWO

Guidelines for Premarital Counseling

———— ❧ ————

A wedding date cannot be confirmed at our church until the couple schedules and completes their first premarital conference with the minister who will perform the wedding. After that conference and if the pastor agrees to perform the wedding on the selected date, the couple's wedding date will be put on the church calendar. At that point, the couple is given a wedding application form (see appendix B) that must be completed and submitted to begin the scheduling process.

Premarital Conference with the Minister

The initial premarital conference between the couple and the minister performing the ceremony is important. This meeting should be held as early in the first stage of wedding planning as possible. In our church, the pastor's confirmation of the saving Christian faith of both the bride and the groom is paramount in the initial counseling session. No couple will be married in our church unless both parties are believers, for only Christian marriages will be performed. This is church policy (see appendix A). If one or both parties are not Christians, the pastor will counsel these individuals in matters of faith, and seek to lead these individuals to a saving knowledge of Jesus Christ.

Once the minister is assured about matters of faith, the couple's responses to the premarital counseling information will be discussed, as well as the meaning of a Christ-filled marriage.

Premarital Counseling Information

Counseling Pastor _____ Marrying Pastor _____

Date of Interview _____ Planned Wedding Date _____

Optional Wedding Date _____

Name of Groom _____ DOB _____

Address _____

Home Phone _____ Work Phone _____ E-mail _____

Christian? _____ Church Member? _____ Where? _____

Name of Bride _____ DOB _____

Address _____

Home Phone _____ Work Phone _____ E-mail _____

Christian? _____ Church Member? _____ Where? _____

Groom

General Background

1. How would the groom describe his family?

2. What is groom's educational background?

3. What is the groom's employment background?

4. How often has the groom moved throughout his life?

Parental Background

1. Are the groom's parents Christians?
2. Do they approve of this relationship and bless it to the point of marriage?

Financial Information

1. Does the groom have a stable and secure financial basis?
2. What indebtedness has the groom incurred? How is he handling indebtedness?
3. Does the groom use credit cards? If so, how?
4   How does the groom handle and manage money?

Health Information

1. When was the groom's last thorough physical exam?
2. Is the groom in good health? Is he free of any communicable disease?

Personal Habits

1. Does the groom smoke or drink?
2. Does the groom use "recreational" drugs?
3. Does the groom gamble?

Spiritual Background

1. Does the groom have a saving knowledge of Jesus Christ?
2. Is the groom maturing in the Christian faith?

3. What is the groom's church history?

Marital Background

1. Has the groom been married and divorced previously?
2. Does the groom have any children? If so, does he have custody of his children?

Dating History

1. What is the groom's dating history?
2. When and how did the groom and bride meet?
3. How would the groom describe their dating life?

Bride

General Background

1. How would the bride describe her family?
2. What is bride's educational background?
3. What is the bride's employment background?
4. How often has the bride moved throughout her life?

Parental Background

1. Are the bride's parents Christians?
2. Do they approve of this relationship and bless it to the point of marriage?

Financial Information

1. Does the bride have a stable and secure financial basis?

2. What indebtedness has the bride incurred? How is she handling indebtedness?

3. Does the bride use credit cards? If so, how?

4. How does the bride handle and manage money?

Health Information

1. When was the bride's last thorough physical exam?

2. Is the bride in good health? Is she free of any communicable disease?

3. Is the bride pregnant?

Personal Habits

1. Does the bride smoke or drink?

2. Does the bride use "recreational" drugs?

3. Does the bride gamble?

Spiritual Background

1. Does the bride have a saving knowledge of Jesus Christ?

2. Is the bride maturing in the Christian faith?

3. What is the bride's church history?

Marital Background

1. Has the bride been married and divorced previously?

2. Does the bride have any children? If so, does she have custody of her children?

Dating Background

1. What is the bride's dating history?

2. When and how did the bride and groom meet?

3. How would the bride describe their dating life?

Both Groom and Bride

Sexual Purity

1. Have they been able to maintain sexual purity in their dating relationship?

2. Discuss their future commitment to sexual purity.

Spiritual Growth

1. Do both desire to grow spiritually?

2. Are both committed to helping each other grow spiritually?

3. Are they planning to be actively involved as a couple in a local church?

Desire for Children

1. Do both desire to have children, if the Lord so blesses?

2. Are they open to adoption, if the Lord so leads?

Careers

1. Do both plan careers outside the home?

2. Do both plan to work when they have children?

Preparation for Marriage Classes

1. Do they plan to attend the preparation-for-marriage classes offered by our church?

2. Discuss these classes, as well as the couple's required participation in premarital counseling.

Wedding Materials

1. Go over the materials in the wedding packet (including: wedding application, wedding handbook, information form for the wedding coordinator, wedding music form, and the couples commitment form).

2. If the couple is ready, have them complete the wedding application (see appendix B), and sign the couples commitment form (see appendix C).

CHAPTER THREE

Guidelines for Preparation-for-Marriage Classes

—— ❧ ——

I t is of paramount importance for couples to receive comprehensive premarital counseling. Most beneficial are multiple counseling sessions with the couple, where they are given "homework" concerning their marital views, family life, and other issues about which to think and questions to answer between sessions. These can be private counseling sessions or preparation-for-marriage classes. The preparation-for-marriage classes may be led by the minister performing the ceremony or by another staff member or lay member of the church.

Our church has established a policy of not allowing couples to be married in our church by one of our pastors without the benefit of extensive premarital counseling. As an established policy of our church and for all of our pastors, this makes the enforcement of this desirable process much more likely to be a reality. When a couple calls our church to set a wedding date, they are informed of this requirement. They are told of premarital counseling classes for which they may sign up and which they will be expected to attend before their wedding date.

Preparation for Marriage Classes

Because of time constraints on our pastoral staff and because of the large volume of weddings held at our church, it has become necessary to offer premarital counseling in the format of classes which are offered periodically. These classes are offered not only to couples engaged to be married, but also to those couples seriously considering the possibility of marriage.

In fact, our church no longer calls these classes "Preparation for Marriage" classes; rather, we have chosen to call them "Is This the Love of Your Life?" In this way, our adult ministry can market these classes to a broader group of people in order to help more couples better prepare for marriage. This has proven quite beneficial in helping counsel couples as to their compatibility or in regard to needed growth areas which need attention before they proceed with marriage.

These preparation-for-marriage classes are held once a week for ten weeks. Each session is two to two-and-a-half hours in length. They are administered and taught by our church's young adult pastoral staff and are offered three times a year. The focus of these classes is relationship building—with one's mate and with God. Couples learn about their relational strengths and identify areas in which they need to grow. Each weekly session has a particular focus. Focal emphases covered in these sessions include:

- Building a Foundation for Oneness
- Grasping God's Plan for Marriage
- Analyzing Expectations and Roles in Marriage
- Understanding Your Past
- Evaluating Your Relationship
- Communicating Effectively with Your Mate
- Dealing with Conflict

- Handling Finances as a Couple
- Preparing for Intimacy
- Recognizing Physiological Differences
- Dealing with In-Laws
- Problem Solving

Before the meeting of the first session, couples are expected to complete a premarital interview (see appendix D). This is submitted as homework at the first class session. Couples who sign up for the preparation-for-marriage classes not only benefit from the evaluation of this premarital interview, but they also profit from personality testing and a relationship assessment. The personality testing provider that our church uses is called "Uniquely You,"[1] which is a national relationship profile service. The relationship assessment service that our church uses is called "Prepare/Enrich."[2] Both resources provide couples with insight about the strengths in their personalities and in their relationships, as well as areas that might prove problematic for marital success.

Following an evaluation of the couple's responses to these assessments, participating couples are taught invaluable skills to help them relate to each other (e.g., skills to increase their assertiveness and self-confidence). Only trained counselors can order and use these assessment materials, but training is easily attainable for those interested in this type of ministry in your church.[3] Certifying lay couples to help with this ministry in your church could provide invaluable service to your church and to the community. This would also be a tremendous help to your church's pastoral staff.

It is through these classes that our couples receive most of the counseling, unless an evaluation of their assessments reveals that they have five or more needed growth areas[4] before they are good candidates for marriage. If this "red flag" situation occurs, a letter is sent to the couple informing them of their assessment results and recommending they postpone marriage plans until they seek counseling for their relationship. Names of professional counselors are provided, since this is beyond the scope of our pastoral services.

There is a charge associated with the preparation-for-marriage course and for the assessments provided. Our church differentiates between the fee charged church members and the fee charged non-church members. This fee is collected in advance, when the couple registers for the preparation-for-marriage course. In addition to these services, the couple receives a marriage workbook[5] which contains outlines of the ten sessions as well as homework assignments for the couple to complete before each session. The couple also receives a recommended reading list for marriage preparation and enrichment.

Our church has one of the most comprehensive preparation-for-marriage programs in our area, so we extend our outreach into the community through these sessions. It is our policy to invite couples outside our church and from other churches to participate. Because of the excellent reputation of our program, we are finding that more and more pastors (from smaller churches which do not have such programs) are sending couples to participate in our premarital sessions. We find that usually 50 percent of the participating couples are not members of our church. We also cooperate with another large church in our city in offering our classes on Wednesdays, if they are going to offer theirs on Sundays, and vice versa. In this way, our two churches have the opportunity to accommodate the needs of more couples.

Bridal Luncheon Seminars

Our church also hosts bridal luncheon seminars. These are open to the community and are offered on a Saturday, twice a year: in the spring and fall. Future brides, their mothers, and any other interested persons are invited to attend these luncheon seminars. In the past we have held this event at our church, but more recently we have rented space at a nearby resort to accommodate the growing numbers. Holding it away from the church is also useful in reaching those who are apprehensive about attending an event held at a church. Like the preparation-for-marriage classes, there is tremendous outreach potential associated with this event. Because of the scope of such an event, it would also be a wonderful joint venture shared by two or more hosting churches.

Our church invites vendors involved with every aspect of wedding planning to set up their displays for these luncheon seminars. Topics of discussion cover everything from selecting wedding invitations to entertaining in the bride's new home, from purchasing the bridal gown to hiring a photographer, from choosing floral arrangements to catering the reception. Those who attend this event learn how to put together a planning notebook, to outline their wedding rehearsal, and to work with a wedding coordinator. Information is also shared on some less obvious topics, including "honeymoon jitters and how to avoid them," as well as ideas for "special evenings for special memories." Questions about manners, etiquette, and appropriate dress for wedding events are addressed.

The vendors also provide us with wonderful door prizes which are given away at the luncheon seminar. There is a charge for this event, and tickets must be purchased in advance.

Nearly/Newlywed Bible Fellowship Classes

In addition to the preparation-for-marriage classes offered by our church, we also offer Sunday morning Bible study classes which target these same couples and newlyweds. We are blessed to have hundreds of couples who are preparing for marriage or who have been married two years or less. They meet each Sunday in various nearly/newlywed classes to learn life-changing principles to help them throughout their married life. The teachers of these classes are dynamic Christian couples in our church. They impart truths about couples' relationships to each other and to God. This is all done in a relaxed and non-threatening environment.

These classes pick up where the preparation-for-marriage sessions leave off. In fact, attendance at one Sunday morning nearly/newlywed Bible study session is one of the homework assignments given in the preparation-for-marriage classes. After attending one of these Sunday morning classes, a high percentage of couples who are not church members join one of these classes and, ultimately, join our church.

CHAPTER FOUR

Guidelines for Wedding Coordinators

———— ✺ ————

The wedding coordinator is an invaluable part of the wedding team of the church. She may be a lay member or staff member of the church. The wedding coordinator should view weddings as a ministry and an outreach of the church. It is vital that the wedding party see and feel the love of Christ demonstrated in this individual. This is especially important since the wedding coordinator may be the only church contact with some of the friends and family members who are unchurched.

The Wedding Plans

The role of the wedding coordinator is to see that the wedding rehearsal and ceremony run as smoothly as possible. She coordinates wedding plans between the wedding party, any outside wedding consultant, the florists, the photographers, the sound technician, the church housekeeping staff, the musicians, and the minister for these events. It is the duty of the wedding coordinator to conduct the wedding rehearsal and to direct the wedding ceremony. In assuming this role, she relieves the minister of these responsibilities.

Our church has more than one wedding coordinator because we have so many weddings held in our facilities. A wedding coordinator is assigned the couple after they have been interviewed by the minister (see chapter 2), and submitted their wedding application to the church (see appendix B)

At the premarital conference with the minister, the couple is given a packet of materials which contains the wedding application, the wedding handbook, an information sheet for the wedding coordinator, the wedding music form, and the couples commitment form. After reading through this information, they telephone the wedding coordinator who answers many of their questions and sets up an appointment with the bride and her mother.

At the scheduled meeting with the bride and her mother, the wedding coordinator makes sure all necessary forms are completed and all the correct information concerning rehearsal and wedding times and locations have been placed on the church calendar. The wedding coordinator also goes over the information supplied by the couple on their completed Information Form for the Wedding Coordinator (see appendix E). In addition to the information requested on this form, it may be helpful for the wedding coordinator to ask:

- Is there anyone in the wedding party who has physical limitations that would require special consideration when being seated or participating in the service?

- If the flower girl or ring bearer is very young, would it be advisable for them to stand throughout the entire ceremony or should they be seated at some point?

- Where should each attendant and groomsman stand? How should they pair up for the recessional?

- If the church does not have a center aisle, which aisle should be used for the processional and which aisle should be used for the recessional?

- Will the bride and groom move from the floor level to the platform level during the ceremony? If so, when?

- Will the bride and groom be using a kneeling bench in the ceremony? If so, when in the ceremony will it be used, and where should it be placed?

- Will there be a unity candle ceremony in the wedding? If so, when in the ceremony will it be used, and where should it be placed?

- Will an aisle runner be used? If so, which groomsmen will be responsible for pulling it, and when should it be pulled?

- Will there be printed programs for the wedding ceremony? If so, who is responsible for handing them out to the guests?

- Is the wedding reception to be held at the church? If so, has the bride and her mother made the appropriate arrangements?

Some wedding coordinators have found that it is helpful to acquire a portfolio of wedding photographs made of weddings in their churches. They have found this helpful in giving the bride ideas about decorations in the church as well as where to place the wedding party. As advertisement, many photographers are willing to furnish wedding coordinators with complimentary wedding photographs taken in their churches. A picture can truly be worth a thousand words when conveying wedding ideas!

Many wedding coordinators keep files on florists, photographers, caterers, instrumentalists, and vocalists who are cooperative in helping with church weddings. Often the bride and her mother ask for such assistance in decision making. This provides the wedding coordinator with another avenue of Christian service to the wedding party.

If the church has candelabra and decorative furnishings available for use in weddings, the wedding coordinator can help the bride and her mother decide which to use, and then record the items requested on their information sheet. Our church has brass altar candelabra, aisle candelabra, and a double kneeling bench available for use in weddings at no charge. We allow only chase candles (to prevent wax spills) to be used in our worship center or chapel. We supply the candles at no charge, but there is a nominal fee charged for the candle wax fillers.

Our church is not obligated to furnish any decorative items not owned by the church; however, we do reserve the right to approve all decorative items obtained from sources outside the church. The wedding coordinator is the one who gives the church's approval for such.

The Wedding Rehearsal

Prior to the wedding rehearsal, the wedding coordinator will make arrangements with the church's custodial staff to make sure they are aware of their responsibilities for the rehearsal and the wedding. She will also coordinate any media support, such as sound or taping.

The wedding coordinator will also remind the bride and her mother of wedding fees and honorariums. All wedding fees should be paid in advance. Our church requires payment of all wedding fees two weeks prior to the wedding.

An order of service for the wedding will be prepared by the wedding coordinator. This will be distributed to all those in the wedding party and those assisting with the wedding prior to or at the beginning of the rehearsal. It is helpful to have everyone assembled at the front of the church to commence the rehearsal on time and in an orderly manner. As important as it is for the rehearsal to begin and end on time, it is even more important to start the rehearsal with prayer. This serves as honor paid to God and as a reminder of the sacredness of the wedding ceremony to the wedding party. The wedding coordinator will go over the order of worship and all procedures with the wedding party as they are seated at the front of the church.

Groomsmen will receive instruction on how to act as ushers for the wedding, on how to seat family members, and on how to light candles. They will also be reminded to pick up their tuxedos, making sure they fit as early as possible. The entire wedding party will be given instructions on the time of arrival for the wedding, as well as dressing room locations. It is helpful to remind the entire wedding party of the importance of being on time for the wedding—at least one hour in advance. This cannot be emphasized too much!

After verbal instructions are given, the wedding party will be placed in their positions and will rehearse the wedding by walking through the order of service. The minister or wedding coordinator will be present to go over the various components of the wedding ceremony. The wedding coordinator usually asks the wedding party to go through the ceremony two times. By then, the wedding party usually has gained confidence in what they are supposed to do.

The presence of musicians at the rehearsal is optional. Our church does not ask the organist to be present for the rehearsal. The vocalists or instrumentalists usually practice with the organist one hour before the wedding. This means that every musician must be well-prepared before the rehearsal. If taped accompaniment is to be used or sound checks are needed, this should be arranged by the musician.

Appropriate decorum of those participating in this service of worship is expected at the rehearsal and the wedding. No one should be allowed to participate in either event if they are under the influence of alcohol or drugs. Likewise, it would be inappropriate for those involved with the wedding to smoke inside the church facilities.

The Wedding Day

On the day of the wedding, the wedding coordinator will arrive early to make sure the church is properly set up and the decorations are in place. She will visit with the bride and her attendants to see if they have everything they need. She will also check with the groom and groomsmen to make certain they are properly dressed and to help them pin on their boutonnieres. The wedding coordinator will confirm that those photographing or videotaping the wedding are correctly placed and know the church's policy on these matters.

The wedding coordinator should remain in the church narthex or foyer until the wedding begins. From that location she is available to answer questions, to handle any problems, and to coordinate the wedding events: ushering, seating of family members, lighting of candles, pulling of aisle runner, processional of the wedding party.

Following the service, the wedding coordinator will assist in coordinating the recessional, in ushering the wedding party, and in helping the wedding party set up for photographs. She should remain at the front of the church to assist the photographer if needed. Also, if designated by the minister to do so, the wedding coordinator will make sure that all of the appropriate signatures are on the wedding license. If a copier is available, she may want to make copies of the wedding license to give to the bride and groom and to keep on file at the church (in case the original gets lost in the mail).

CHAPTER FIVE

Guidelines for Planning Wedding Ceremonies

———— ❧ ————

Christian weddings are not only occasions for celebration; they are also services of worship. Because these services are often held in churches, this serves as an effective reminder of the sacredness of the marital ceremony. All that is done in a wedding ceremony should focus the attention of those who are participating in the wedding, as well as those attending the wedding, primarily on God. To many this sounds odd, for the attention always seems to be placed on the bride and groom. Should they not be the primary focus of this big event in their lives?

The answer is no. Their importance is secondary, and the primary emphasis rests solely on what God has done and is doing in their lives. In the service of marriage, God is to be honored above all others. God is to be acknowledged with all reverence. God is to be worshiped with true devotion. God is to be blessed by everything that happens in this sacred hour. Without him, there could be no true love. Without him, there could be no marriage. Without him, there could be no hope for this couple's future life together. He is invited to be present as special guest, sovereign Lord, steadfast Friend, and sure Guide.

Planning the Christian Wedding Ceremony

It is exciting to plan a service of marriage! It is exciting for the bride and groom, for their parents, for the minister, for the wedding coordinator, for the musicians. All involved realize that this is a life-changing event. If it is a Christian marriage, they should also realize the sacredness of this event. They should desire that the ceremony reflect the couple's love and commitment for each other and for God.

It is important for those planning the ceremony to remember that Christian weddings are celebrations of the character of God. Christian weddings are celebrations of the acts of God. Christian weddings are celebrations of the person of God—above all others present. It is, therefore, important that every aspect of the wedding ceremony bring honor and glory to God. Christian weddings should not elevate human love above divine love. Christian weddings should not elevate that which is secular above that which is sacred. God's Word, more than any etiquette book, is truly authoritative for weddings. His Word should be read. His Word should be taught. His Word should be sung.

How should those involved plan a marriage service? There are several possible approaches.

Choosing the Traditional Wedding

The couple may desire a traditional ceremony (see ceremonies 1 and 2) and wish to follow a standard order of service for their wedding. They would express this to the minister when they have a conference with him. The minister would ask if they prefer a truly traditional wedding with all the "thee's" and "thou's" (see ceremony 2 vows) or a more modern version of the traditional wedding (see ceremony 1 vows). The minister would also ask if they have a favorite passage of Scripture and, if so, the minister would probably use that scriptural passage in developing and writing a wedding charge or statement of marriage for the service.

If they have no scriptural preference, the minister can use the standard wedding charge or statement of marriage or select one from another ceremony in this book. Then, when the couple meets with the organist and expresses their desire for music, the wedding music may be selected and placed in the designated spots in the order of worship.

Selecting a Thematic Wedding

I have tried to personalize the weddings that I have performed over the years. I have found that selecting a wedding theme, much like choosing a sermon topic, is a meaningful way to begin shaping the wedding ceremony to be a reflection of the love the couple has for each other and for God. In this book, most of the ceremonies are thematic (see ceremonies 3–20). These ceremonies and their vows are planned around a common theme, taken from Scripture or life circumstances (e.g., partners who have been previously married, perhaps with their children involved). The theme is reflected in multiple parts of the ceremony, especially in the statement of marriage and in the vows. The couple may also desire to carry out a chosen theme with the music that is selected.

In planning the components of a wedding ceremony with a couple, it is helpful to know if a couple has an idea about a biblically oriented theme or a favorite passage of Scripture they would like to see included in the ceremony. As previously stated, this may provide a starting point for the development of the statement of marriage and vows. Excellent biblical themes for weddings include: home, family, love, honor, faithfulness, oneness, friendship, relationships, covenant, promise, blessing, treasure/gift, weddings in the Bible, wedding songs in the Bible, roles in marriage, words spoken in marriage, purpose/goals of marriage.

Once a theme has been selected, appropriate Scripture is selected to further magnify the Lord through theme development in the writing of the statement of marriage and wedding vows. Once these elements are in place, the rest of the ceremony can be written or selected from other sources.

Writing an Original Wedding

More and more couples are choosing to write their wedding vows, prayers, and other parts of the wedding ceremony. How should a couple begin? If using this book, a couple should read through the various ceremonies included in this volume. They may decide either to write original portions of the ceremony and/or to adapt various elements from ceremonies in this book.

For example, a couple may like one part of one ceremony and several parts from another ceremony. They may want a unity candle ceremony when none is indicated or may not desire to pray at a kneeling bench when it is indicated in this book. They should begin by outlining their wedding ceremony. What elements do they want included? Can they find these aspects of the wedding ceremony already written? If so, they may "cut and paste" these to form their ceremony or, perhaps, make revisions in the written ceremonies.

The rule of order for utilizing this book is that there are no rules, except that God be honored and worshiped above all others. Remember, none of these ceremonies are "written in stone." Various parts of ceremonies may be deleted and other things easily included. Be creative! It will be helpful to look through the entire book to find the various parts which best suit those involved. Then an original ceremony utilizing whatever aspects best reflect the love and commitment of the couple can be created.

The Importance of Wedding Vows

The making of vows is a serious act of faith and commitment for Christians, especially those vows, or oaths,[1] made in marriage. The marriage vow is a solemn promise made to one mate's and before God. It is permanent and binding. As with covenants, the keeping of a vow is associated with blessing, whereas the breaking of it precipitates God-imposed consequences. Wedding vows are very personal in nature. They should be. They should reflect the love and commitment of the bride and groom. Wedding vows reflect the relationship of the couple with God. Wedding vows also reflect the relationship of the couple with each other, usually expressing either an equalitarian or hierarchical view of the role of the husband and wife in marriage.

The Significance of Wedding Music and Musicians

The music selected for a wedding should enhance the worship and adoration of God. Again, it is important to remember the primary focus of the marriage ceremony is on God and what he is doing in and through the lives of the couple. The lyrics of wedding songs should reflect this. The choice of songs, therefore, should be sacred and not secular. Popular secular songs are not appropriate selections for the ceremony. (The reception would provide a better time and place to enjoy favorite secular songs that, of course, reflect good taste.) Our church does not allow the use of popular secular music at weddings in our worship center or chapel.

How does a person know what music to select and what music is appropriate? It is always wise to ask someone associated with weddings at the church. While the wedding coordinator and the minister can provide help in this area, the church organist usually is the one who can best advise a couple. The organist can help the couple select the music played or sung prior to the service (the prelude); music when the grandmothers and mothers are seated; the processional; music during the service (a congregational hymn at the beginning of the service, a vocal selection at the conclusion of the ring ceremony, a vocal selection during the time of prayer, a vocal selection during the lighting of the unity candle, a choral benediction); the recessional; and music at the end of the service as guests are leaving (the postlude).

There is great variety, reflecting many styles and degrees of difficulty, in Christian wedding music (see appendix F). The organist who plays for weddings can be an invaluable source of ideas for the couple when making music selections.

While the careful selection of wedding music is important, the wise choice of musicians is equally important. The musicians for a wedding should be chosen prayerfully, as they have a sacred ministry within the worship service. They, too, must understand the purpose of Christian marriage. They must agree to abide by the wedding policies of the church as well as submit to the authority of the minister performing the service and to the direction of the wedding coordinator. Organists should be thoroughly familiar with the instrument they will play prior to the service. Vocalists may need to rehearse with the organist/instrumentalists and to work with the sound technician ahead of time. Musicians normally receive a fee set by the church or an appropriate honorarium for their service.

The church may require the couple to let them know about the music to be used and the names of the wedding musicians in advance of the wedding. The wedding coordinator also needs this information. This is also necessary for the printing of wedding programs. Our church requires the couple to complete a wedding music form and submit it to the music office no later than two months before the wedding (see appendix G).

The Individuality of Wedding Programs

Many couples choose to prepare a wedding program to be printed and distributed to wedding guests. While these programs usually contain certain common elements, they should reflect the individual personality, faith, commitment, love, and taste of the couple involved. A couple's wedding program should serve as a lasting memento of their special day.

A wedding program usually includes the order of service, the names of those in the wedding party, and any personal notes the couple chooses to write. Wedding programs should also include the words to any congregational hymns or choruses as well as responsive readings. It often contains a passage of Scripture. If their wedding is thematic in its components, the couple may choose to write a brief explanation of their choice of theme and its biblical basis. Some wedding programs contain a poem, a prayer, a picture of the couple, and/or the couple's new address. The minister, musicians, and wedding coordinator can help the couple in preparing the program. They often have on file copies of former wedding ceremonies that they can show the couple.

PART 2

Wedding Ceremonies

———— ⚜ ————

A New Tradition

A Ceremony for a Modern, Traditional Wedding

———— ❧ ————

THE PRELUDE

THE SEATING OF THE MOTHERS

(Before the groom's mother is seated, she and the groom's father will light the groom's individual unity candle. Likewise, before the bride's mother is seated, she and the bride's father will light the bride's individual unity candle.)

THE PROCESSIONAL

THE WELCOME

Dear family and friends, we are gathered here today in the sight of God and in the presence of this company to witness the union of _____ (groom) and _____ (bride) in Christian marriage. Marriage is a holy estate given by God to fulfill us as individuals and as a couple, and to conform us, as maturing believers, into the image of Christ. (*Optional sentence:* _____ (groom) and _____ (bride) have chosen to be married in the Lord's house as a testimony of their faith in God and as a witness to all present that they desire to honor their Lord and Savior in their lives and in their home.[1]) May our heavenly Father look down upon this event with his favor. May the Lord, Jesus Christ, be present and add his blessing. May the Holy Spirit attend and seal these vows in love.[2]

THE GIVING IN MARRIAGE

In God's most amazing act of creation, he created beings in his own image. They not only were made to reflect his image, but they were made in his image. We read of this astonishing event in the first chapter of Genesis: "So God created man in his own image, in the image of God he created him; male and female he created them" (v. 27). Being made in the image of the triune God, the male was not complete when he was alone, so God created the perfect complement for the male: the female. She was to be his life companion, his colaborer in fulfilling the creation mandate of God: "Be fruitful and increase in number; fill the earth and subdue it. Rule over the fish of the sea and the birds of the air and over every living creature that moves on the ground" (v. 28).

In the time of man's innocence, God instituted the estate of matrimony between the first man and the first woman. Marriage was consecrated by God, not only for mutual help and comfort, but also as a means of procreation. In marriage, God gave his creatures, man and woman, the ability—and the mandate—to create life like themselves, life in the image of God. Not only this, but God also gave this first couple a taste of redemption for mankind, as marriage is a foretaste of the mystical union that exists between Christ and his bride, the church.

It is into this holy estate that _____ (groom) and _____ (bride) have chosen to enter. Not knowing any just reason that these two should not be married, I ask, "Who gives this woman to be married to this man?"

Father responds: "Her mother and I do."

(Alternate: *Father and mother respond:* "We do.")

THE INVOCATION

Let us pray: Father-Creator, we thank you for your wondrous and gracious creation of mankind in your image. We thank you for the heavenly character of love—especially when *your* love exists between a man and a woman. We thank you for your institution of marriage and of the joy and the sense of completion that it brings. We thank you for our redemption in Jesus Christ, as we are made new creatures in him. We ask now that you bless the union of _____ (groom) and _____ (bride) that they may grow to conform to the image of their Lord and Savior, Jesus Christ. We ask you to enable this couple to bless you in their lives and in their marriage in all the days ahead. For it is in your name alone that we pray. Amen.

THE STATEMENT OF MARRIAGE

_____ (groom) and _____ (bride), you are about to pledge the most sacred vows that one person makes with another. As you stand before the witness of God and this company, it is important that you give careful consideration to that which you are promising. You are accountable to your precious mate and to God for that which you pledge. It is advisable that you soberly examine the vows you are about to make.

These vows, which you have selected to represent your commitment, are very traditional, yet timeless in the earnest promises they reflect. In these few moments, we will examine the three things that you are vowing to do for your mate, regardless of life's circumstances, for as long as you live.

Your first promise is *to honor your mate*. What does "to honor" mean? As Christians, we look to God's Word for instruction on this and other important matters. In doing so, we find that *honor* is a biblical term for respect, esteem, high regard, and reward. In its various forms, it is found more than 222 times in the English Bible. Honor is used to represent respect paid to superiors, such as God, Christ, the emperor, church officers, the elderly, or parents. Honor can also be something bestowed as a reward for virtuous behavior, such as for honoring God or serving Christ, for manifesting wisdom, discipline, or righteousness.

To honor someone or something is to acknowledge and show respect for the authority or worthiness of the object of one's honor.[3] This is the connotation of "to honor" one's mate. As you make your vows to each other, you are pledging to acknowledge and to show respect for the worthiness of your mate. Showing honor to your mate involves an affective side (that is, a feeling of respect for your mate) and outward manifestations (that is, your actions toward or regarding your mate). Tragically, there are too few marriage partners who consistently keep this vow. This lack of honoring one's mate contributes significantly to troubled and failed marriages. Too often marriage partners fail to realize the value and worthiness of the one they profess to love above all others. Instead, they tend to elevate their own selves or others to the demotion of their mate.

There is one other aspect of honoring your mate about which you should be aware. In the Bible the word *love* is sometimes used as a synonym for *honor*. This is seen when Paul tells the Romans to "love one another with mutual affection; outdo one another in showing honor" (Rom. 12:10, NRSV). _____ (groom) and _____ (bride), if you truly love each other, you will desire to honor each other. We see also in Scripture the highest example of such honor. It is the example of Christ. In washing the disciples' feet, he paid them the honor of service, of subjecting his own priorities to their interests.[4] _____ (groom) and _____ (bride), do you really love each other enough to honor each other as Christ would have you do? Are you prepared to follow Christ's example by subjecting your personal priorities to the other's best interest and serving the other all the days of your life?

Next, you will promise *to love and to cherish your mate*. For two people like you, who are so deeply in love, these promises sound easy enough to keep. Yet there are many who start out "in love" when they marry, but who apparently no longer "cherish" their mate enough to stay married for a lifetime. We hear the statistics; we see the marital casualties of our day. Do not despair, however; you can build a stable and loving relationship that will withstand the storms of life. How is that possible?

You must look to your heavenly Father, not only for his wise counsel on marriage, but also for his being a role model of loving and cherishing this new family member. God's Word, in 1 John, describes his role modeling: "How great is the love the Father has lavished on us, that we should be called children of God! And that is what we are!" (3:1). It is amazing that God Almighty chose to adopt us as his children—not his servants—his family members! This lavish love is unconditional and blind to sinful shortcomings. As you are about to "adopt" this new family member, your mate, remember to lavish on your mate godly, unconditional love. This is much more than simply saying the words, *I love you,* everyday. First John continues by saying, "Dear children, let us not love with words or tongue but with actions and in truth. . . . Let us love one another, for love comes from God. . . . we know and rely on the love God has for us. God is love. Whoever lives in love lives in God, and God in him" (3:18; 4:7*a*, 16).

These verses explain to us that God is not only the source of love; he *is* love. If you are to live all your married days "in love," then you must do as the verse says, "Whoever lives in love lives in God, and God in him" (4:16*c*). It cannot be with just your words or even your well-intentioned vows that you proclaim your love to and for your mate. Your words must be clothed in action, day after day, from the little things to the big things of life. This involves a total commitment of your life—to live *in* God and allowing God to live *in* you—so that your relationship to him and to your mate reflects his love. This means your focus cannot be on attaining the perfect house or the great job but rather, on maintaining the humble posture of a loving servant who is willing to serve his God and serve his mate . . . for life! Then—and only then—can you begin to understand what *to cherish* means.

In this insightful book of the Bible, we find: "This is how we know what to love and to cherish is: Jesus Christ laid down his life for you. And you ought to lay down your life for your mate" (1 John 3:16, paraphrased). _____ (groom) and _____ (bride), you must lay down your lives—your selfish desires, passions, ambition, and pride—for each other. You must cherish the other more than you cherish your own self. Your mate now comes first—before yourself, before your parents, before your friends, before your job, before your leisure activities, before your caring for your own exhaustion and needs at the end of a hard day. You must serve each other as Christ served. Then and only then will you truly fulfill your vow "to love and to cherish." And all of this wonderfully ties into honoring your mate.

THE VOWS

_____ (groom) and _____ (bride), you have listened to this sobering explanation of the meaning of the vows you are about to make. These vows are as binding in adversity as they are in prosperity. They should be broken only by death. If you are prepared to make such a serious commitment, will you now turn, face one another, and join hands.

_____ (groom), in taking _____ (bride) to be your wife, do you so promise to honor, to love, and to cherish her in sickness as in health, in poverty as in wealth, in hardship as in blessing, until death alone shall part you?

Groom responds: "I do."

_____ (bride), in taking _____ (groom) to be your husband, do you so promise to honor, to love, and to cherish him in sickness as in health, in poverty as in wealth, in hardship as in blessing, until death alone shall part you?

Bride responds: "I do."

THE EXCHANGE OF RINGS

You will now seal your vows, "to honor, to love, to cherish," by the giving and receiving of rings. The unbroken circles of these rings symbolize a union between husband and wife with God that cannot be broken. This is in accord with God's creation plan, and it brings honor to the One who created you to glorify him. The precious glistening gold of these rings symbolizes all that is pure and holy in the marital bond. As these metals were refined to fashion these beautiful rings, may God ever refine and purify you both as new creations in Christ Jesus. As you wear these rings, may they ever remind you of your love and of the commitment you made this day.

_____ (groom), place this ring on _____'s (bride's) finger and repeat after me:

Groom: "I, _____ (groom), take you, _____ (bride), to be my wedded wife to have and to hold, from this day forward. I pledge before God and these witnesses to place your good above mine, now and always, no matter the circumstances. I promise to honor you, to love you, and to cherish you until death do us part. Joyfully and willingly, I commit myself to you, and to you alone."

_____ (bride), place this ring on _____'s (groom's) finger and repeat after me:

Bride: "I, _____ (bride), take you, _____ (groom), to be my wedded husband to have and to hold, from this day forward. I pledge before God and these witnesses to place your good above mine, now and always, no matter the circumstances. I promise to honor you, to love you, and to cherish you until death do us part. Joyfully and willingly, I commit myself to you, and to you alone."

THE SONG

(Song to be sung as the bride and groom kneel in prayer.)

THE PRAYER

(The bride and groom will continue kneeling in prayer.)

Gracious Father, thank you for creating us in your image. Because of this, we are able to know you and to know what true love is. We see in this couple a deep and abiding love for each other and for you. We have witnessed the giving of vows and rings in this sacred hour. Through your power and blessing, we ask you to enable these two to keep their vows, to be renewed daily in their love and commitment, to walk in mutual faith, to build a strong and lasting marriage, and to live by confidence in your grace. As they grow in conformity to Christ's image, may you, O Lord, receive glory through the lives and marriage of _____ (groom) and _____ (bride). In Jesus' name we pray. Amen.

(The bride and groom will stand.)

THE LIGHTING OF THE UNITY CANDLE

_____ (groom) and _____ (bride), your parents have lighted a separate candle for each of you. They did so to symbolize your individual lives and the families from which you come. Your individual lives have been a blessing to your parents who have received immeasurable joy in seeing you grow and mature over the years. Your individual lives have been a blessing to those who have known and loved you. Your individual lives have been a blessing to God whom you have faithfully served.

As you lift your individual candles from their holders, be reminded that marriage does not eliminate your separate identities. You are made in the image of your heavenly Father; nevertheless, you are each unique. God has created you as such for his purpose and his glory. You will not extinguish your individual candles, as God still has much to do in and through your individual lives. Together you will light the unity candle to symbolize your union in marriage. Together you assume a new identity—as one with each other and the Lord. Today, God has created anew in you a union that will enable you to fulfill his creation mandate to serve him in the world and to establish a family.

THE SONG

(Song to be played or sung during the lighting of the unity candle.)

THE DECLARATION OF MARRIAGE

_____ (groom) and _____ (bride), we have witnessed the pledging of your love and commitment to each other. We have seen the sealing of your solemn vows of marriage by the giving and receiving of rings. It is, therefore, my joy and privilege to declare you husband and wife. _____ (groom), you may kiss your bride.

THE INTRODUCTION OF THE NEWLYWEDS

Friends and family of the bride and groom, it is my pleasure to present to you Mr. and Mrs. _____.

THE RECESSIONAL

THE POSTLUDE

A Classic Wedding

A Ceremony for a Classic, Very Traditional Wedding

———— ✿ ————

THE PROCESSIONAL

THE WELCOME

Dearly beloved, we are gathered together here in the sight of God, and in the presence of this company, to join together this man and this woman in holy matrimony, which is commended by the apostle Paul to be honorable among all men; and, therefore, is not by any to be entered into unadvisedly or lightly, but reverently, discreetly, advisedly, and in the fear of God. Into this holy estate, these two persons come now to be joined. (*The following statement is optional:* If any man can show just cause why they may not lawfully be joined together, let him now speak, or else, hereafter, forever hold his peace.)

THE CHARGE

_____ (groom), wilt thou have this woman to be thy wedded wife, to live together after God's ordinance in the holy estate of matrimony? Wilt thou love her, comfort her, and keep her, in sickness and in health; and forsaking all others, keep thee only unto her, so long as you both shall live?

Groom responds: "I will."

_____ (bride), wilt thou have this man to be thy wedded husband, to live together after God's ordinance in the holy estate of matrimony? Wilt thou love him, comfort him and keep him, in sickness and in health; and forsaking all others, keep thee only unto him, so long as you both shall live?

Bride responds: "I will."

THE GIVING OF THE BRIDE

Who giveth this woman to be married to this man?

Father responds: "I do," "We do," or, "Her mother and I do." *(The father is then seated.)*

THE STATEMENT OF MARRIAGE

_____ (groom) and _____ (bride), as part of your marriage ceremony, you have chosen to use what has been known as "the traditional wedding vows." They can be traced back to the 1300s in England, yet they have remained, perhaps, the most loved and best known of all ceremonies. In these moments, before you take your vows, let's go further back than the 1300s. Let's travel back in time to the first wedding and look at that original match. We will seek the answer to the question some people ask, "Why do people get married?" God answers that for us in his Word.

As we examine the creation events in the first chapter of Genesis, we discover the triune God saying, "Let us make man in our own image, in our likeness, and let them rule over the fish of the sea and the birds of the air, over the livestock, over all the earth, and over all the creatures that move along the ground. So God created man in his own image, in the image of God he created him; male and female he created them" (Gen. 1:26–27). God created male and female and joined them together as a *demonstration* of himself. When a couple is united in the oneness of marriage, God is glorified, and the divine image of the heavenly Father is reflected on earth.

The creation account tells us more about the importance of the union of man and woman. We know that marriage is important because it was God's plan for the *elevation* of a new kind of creation, one that was superior to all else God had created. God told man to rule over his magnificent creation: "Fill the earth and subdue it. Rule over the fish of the sea and the birds of the air and over every living creature that moves on the ground" (Gen. 1:28).

As we examine the second chapter of Genesis, we find that God made marriage as the *completion* of his supreme creature, man. Adam lived in a perfect environment and had a fascinating creation to observe, but still something was missing. God, ever sensitive to his creature's needs, said, "It is not good for the man to be alone. I will make a helper suitable for him" (Gen. 2:18). Was God successful? The first recorded words of Adam were: "This is now bone of my bones" (Gen. 2:23*a*). The Living Bible paraphrases his words as: "This is it!" Adam finally knew the satisfaction of being complete.

In the Academy Award-winning movie *Rocky,* the boxing champion had a love relationship with a woman named Adrian. Her brother, Pauly, couldn't understand it. "I don't see it," he said. "What's the attraction?" To which Rocky responded, "I don't know . . . fills gaps, I guess." Pauly asked, "What gaps?" "She's got gaps, I got gaps," Rocky explained. "Together we fill gaps."[1]

Another reason we marry may be discovered in Genesis. We read that God made marriage for the *reproduction* of a godly heritage. "God blessed them and said to them, 'Be fruitful and increase in number'" (Gen. 1:28). Godly children are a gift from God. "Children are a gift from the LORD; The fruit of the womb is a reward" (Ps. 127:3, NASB).

Marriage, simply defined, is the contemplation of the love of God in and through the form of other human beings—the spouse and the child.[2]

Believing that you understand something of the reason for marriage as God has revealed it, are you ready now to confirm your commitment to God and to each other in Christian marriage?

Couple responds: "We are."

THE VOWS

_____ (groom) and _____ (bride), join hands and repeat after me:

Groom: "I, _____ (groom), take thee, _____ (bride), to be my wedded wife, to have and to hold from this day forward, for better, for worse, for richer, for poorer, in sickness and in health; to love and to cherish, till death do us part; according to God's holy ordinance; and, thereto, I plight (or pledge) thee my troth."

Bride: "I, _____ (bride), take thee, _____ (groom), to be my wedded husband, to have and to hold from this day forward, for better, for worse, for richer, for poorer, in sickness and in health; to love, to cherish, and obey till death do us part; according to God's holy ordinance; and, thereto, I plight (or pledge) thee my troth."

THE EXCHANGE OF RINGS

_____ (groom), is there a ring?

Groom responds: "Yes."

(The minister takes the ring from the best man or ring bearer and places it in the groom's hand. The groom will then place the ring on the third finger of the bride's left hand. The groom, still holding the ring in place, repeats the following vow.)

_____ (groom), repeat after me:

Groom: "With this ring I thee wed, and with all my worldly goods I thee endow. In the name of the Father, and of the Son, and of the Holy Ghost. Amen."

_____ (bride), is there a ring?

Bride responds: "Yes."

(The minister takes the ring from the maid or matron of honor and places it in the bride's hand. The bride will then place the ring on the third finger of the groom's left hand. The bride, still holding the ring in place, repeats the following vow.)

_____ (bride), repeat after me:

Bride: "With this ring I thee wed, and with all my worldly goods I thee endow. In the name of the Father, and of the Son, and of the Holy Ghost. Amen."

THE LORD'S PRAYER

Congregation, please join us in praying our Lord's Prayer: "Our Father, who art in heaven, hallowed be thy name. Thy kingdom come; thy will be done on earth as it is in heaven. Give us this day our daily bread. And forgive us our trespasses as we forgive those who trespass against us. And lead us not into temptation, but deliver us from evil. For thine is the kingdom, and the power, and the glory forever" (Matt. 6:9–13, modified KJV).

(Minister continues praying): O Eternal God, Creator and Preserver of all mankind, Giver of all spiritual grace, the Author of everlasting life, send your blessing upon these, your servants, _____ (groom) and _____ (bride), whom we bless in thy name. May they live faithfully together as husband and wife, and keep the solemn vows made between them, which are symbolized by the rings given and received. May this couple ever remain in perfect love and peace together, and live according to thy laws. Through Jesus Christ, our Lord. Amen.

THE PRONOUNCEMENT

Forasmuch as _____ (groom) and _____ (bride) have consented together in holy wedlock, and have witnessed the same before God and this company, and, hereto, have given and pledged their troth, each to the other, and have declared the same by giving and receiving a ring, and by joining hands, I pronounce that they are husband and wife. In the name of the Father, and of the Son, and of the Holy Ghost. Amen.

THE BENEDICTION

_____ (groom) and _____ (bride), "The LORD bless you, and keep you; The LORD make His face shine on you, And be gracious to you; The LORD lift up His countenance on you, And give you peace" (Num. 6:24–26 NASB). Amen.

THE PRESENTATION

_____ (groom), you may kiss your wife. I am pleased to announce for the first time, "This is Mr. and Mrs. _____ ." What God hath joined together, let not man put asunder.

THE RECESSIONAL

The Family Blessing

A Ceremony for Confirming the Family Blessing on a Marriage

———— ❦ ————

THE PROCESSIONAL

THE INVOCATION

God most high, blessed be your glorious name![1] We bless you as God, the King of kings, the Lord of lords, the blessed and only Ruler.[2] We praise you, because you have promised that the man is blessed whose sin the Lord will never count against him.[3] We are blessed, because our salvation is in you.[4] We lift your name on high, for you alone are our strength,[5] our refuge,[6] and our peace.[7] You have given us your Word that you bless the home of the righteous.[8] With those assurances, do bless now this joyous occasion with your heavenly blessing. In the name of the source of all blessings, Jesus Christ, our Lord. Amen.

THE RESPONSIVE READING

(Program will be necessary for congregation to participate)

Congregation, please stand and join me as we read responsively this blessing:

Minister and
Congregation: Bless the Lord, oh my soul, and all that is within me, bless his holy Name!

Minister: Lord, bless this union of _____ (groom) and _____ (bride). May they strive to please you in all they do. May their marriage glorify you, our Lord and our Savior.

Congregation: Bless the Lord, and forget not all his benefits.

Minister: Lord, bless _____ (groom). Bless him as he assumes this new role as _____'s (bride's) cherished husband. Bless him as he seeks to become the life partner who will be a blessing to his wife. Bless him as he matures in his walk with you and as he strives to do your will.

Congregation: Bless the Lord, and forget not all his benefits.

Minister: Lord, bless _____ (bride). Bless her as she assumes this new role as _____'s (groom's) cherished wife. Bless her as she seeks to become the life partner who will be a blessing to her husband. Bless her as she matures in her walk with you and as she strives to do your will.

Congregation: Bless the Lord, and forget not all his benefits.

Minister: Lord, may they never make the mistake of merely living for each other. May they, as a united couple, together join hands to worship and serve you. Show them their great spiritual purpose in life.

Congregation: Bless the Lord, and forget not all his benefits.

Minister: Lord, bless _____ (groom) and _____ (bride). When the sun sets on this blessed day, may they be found still hand in hand, very proud of each other, and closer to you. May they always offer praise to you for each other, until, at last, one shall lay the other in your heavenly arms.

**Minister and
Congregation:**   Bless the Lord, oh my soul, and all that is within me, bless his holy Name!

CONGREGATIONAL SONG

Bless the Lord, O My Soul

(At the conclusion of the song, instruct the congregation to be seated.)

THE MARRIAGE DISCOURSE

We are here today to ask God's blessing on _____'s (groom's) and _____'s (bride's) marriage. Our greatest desire is to honor the Lord and bless him in this sacred time together. We come today to give honor and glory due our Master, Lord, and King. The psalmist wrote: "Praise the LORD. Praise, O servants of the LORD, praise the name of the LORD. Let the name of the LORD be praised, both now and forevermore. From the rising of the sun to the place where it sets, the name of the LORD is to be praised. The LORD is exalted over all the nations, his glory above the heavens" (Ps. 113:1–4).

The Bible teaches that marriage should exemplify the relationship of Christ with his church, with that relationship being primarily a spiritual relationship. The union of spirits is the foundation of the marriage, not a secondary afterthought. Psalm 127 declares: "Unless the LORD builds the house, its builders labor in vain. Unless the LORD watches over the city, the watchmen stand guard in vain" (v. 1). In your marriage you must seek him, trust him, and always turn to him. Your marriage must be a fortress where both parties are united with God in seeking to keep out any enemies who would attack or destroy it.

Today we want to commit you, _____ (groom) and _____ (bride), to the Lord. We want to bless you in this sacred hour. To bless someone in the Old Testament was a very special act. In Genesis, we find these words of Isaac when he blessed Jacob: "May God give you of the dew of heaven, and of the fatness of the earth" (Gen. 27:28 NKJV). Years later, when Jacob blessed his sons and grandchildren, he began by saying, "May the God . . . who has been my shepherd all my life to this day . . . bless these boys" (48:15*b*–16*b*). In this scriptural passage, we discover one reason why they called on God to confirm their child's blessing: they were sure of God's commitment and faithfulness to them.

Wise parents will model the practice of bestowing the blessing on their children. _____ (bride's father) and _____ (bride's mother) have publicly and privately blessed _____ (bride) in many ways for many years. Now they come to bless _____ (bride) and her husband today. Remember God remains changeless. He desires to bless us and give us strength. Likewise, _____ (groom's father) and _____ (groom's mother) have publicly and privately blessed _____ (groom) in many ways for many years. Now they come to bless _____ (groom) and his wife today.

Also, remember our heavenly Father desires to bless us and give us strength. These wise parents, in committing their children and their marriage to the Lord, taught them that God is intimately concerned with their life and welfare. These wise parents, in stressing the fact that the Lord is interested in their being blessed, whether single or married, introduced them to Someone who can, and will, be their best Friend and personal Encourager and to whom they can draw close throughout their lives.

In Genesis 48 and 49, we read that Jacob (called "Israel") pronounced a blessing for each of his twelve sons and two of his grandchildren. After he finished blessing each child, we read: "He blessed them, giving each the blessing appropriate to him" (Gen. 49:28*b*).

In a few moments, _____ (groom) and _____ (bride), after you make your vows to each other and seal your commitment with the giving of rings, your parents will be coming forward to pass on to each of you the blessing which is appropriate. In doing so, they will be commending you to live faithfully before God, to trust always in his care and in his blessing of your lives and marriage, and to establish your home as one that evidences lives of faith and divine love.

THE MARRIAGE VOWS

_____ (groom), will you face _____ (bride) and repeat these vows:

Groom: "It is my heart's desire to be a blessing to you, _____ (bride). It is more blessed to give than to receive, and I covenant with you that I will always strive to be a giver in our marriage. I commit to partnering with you in making our home a blessing. I love you with a love only Christ could place within my heart. I will encourage you, pray with you, and join you in serving God. I will keep my vows as long as we both shall live. I do so promise."

Bride: "It is my heart's desire to be a blessing to you, _____ (groom). It is more blessed to give than to receive, and I covenant with you that I will always strive to be a giver in our marriage. I commit to partnering with you in making our home a blessing. I love you with a love only Christ could place within my heart. I will encourage you, pray with you, and join you in serving God. I will keep my vows as long as we both shall live. I do so promise."

THE MARRIAGE RINGS

The rings you are about to give are precious symbols of the vows you have made. Share them now as tangible reminders of the blessing of God's promise in your lives and of the blessing of fulfilling your promises made today. Repeat after me:

Groom: "_____ (bride), this ring is yours. It is given with my heart's desire to be faithful to my vows. I give it with the deepest gratitude that Christ has blessed me by giving you to me. Amen."

Bride: "_____ (groom), this ring is yours. It is given with my heart's desire to be faithful to my vows. I give it with the deepest gratitude that Christ has blessed me by giving you to me. Amen."

THE MARRIAGE BLESSING

_____ (groom) and _____ (bride), you are both truly blessed beyond measure for the godly heritage that is yours. You have been raised in the love and fear of the Lord. You have been taught to walk in the ways of truth and righteousness. As you have matured in years, you have also matured in the faith. You both have conveyed to me the overwhelming desire to express the debt of gratitude that you owe your parents for the blessing of faithfulness they have shown in raising you as children of God in the family of faith.

_____ (groom) and _____ (bride) ask that their parents now join in standing with them. *(The bride and groom will pronounce their blessings without the prompting of the minister.)*

Groom (addressing his parents): _____ (Mom or other name), _____ (Dad or other name), in the presence of our family and friends, I want to thank you for the sacrificial love you have shown me during my entire life. I want to bless you both for your great faith and your great faithfulness in raising me in the love and fear of the Lord. I want to praise God for giving me wonderful Christian parents like you. I know that I am who I am, as a child of God and a follower of Christ, because of the rich heritage of faith that you have passed on to me.

Groom (addressing the bride's parents): _____ (Mom or other name), _____ (Dad or other name), thank you for making me feel like one of your family. Thank you for raising your daughter to be a wonderful and godly woman. I pledge to you that I will love and cherish _____ (bride's name) for as long as I live.

(The bride will now repeat the words of the groom or some variation of these words:)

Bride (addressing her parents): _____ (Mom or other name), _____ (Dad or other name), in the presence of our family and friends, I want to thank you for the sacrificial love you have shown me during my entire life. I want to bless you both for your great faith and your great faithfulness in raising me in the love and fear of the Lord. I want to praise God for giving me wonderful Christian parents like you. I know that I am who I am, as a child of God and a follower of Christ, because of the rich heritage of faith that you have passed on to me.

Bride (addressing the groom's parents): _____ (Mom or other name), _____ (Dad or other name), thank you for making me feel like one of your family. Thank you for raising your son to be a wonderful and godly man. I pledge to you that I will love and cherish _____ (groom's name) for as long as I live.

Groom (addressing both sets of parents): _____ (bride) and I want you, our wonderful parents, to know that we love you. We thank you for countless times you have prayed for us and our future mate. We ask your continued prayers and wise support for us as we try to become a family exhibiting all the wonderful qualities we have both come to know and appreciate in our homes. You will always be a part of our lives. We welcome you at all times to our home. May God bless you and always keep you in his loving care.

Minister: What a blessing it is to see the living out of what God ordained families to be! Knowing the great love that _____ (groom) and _____ (bride) have for each other and for the Lord, and knowing that they have sought his will in their relationship with each other, it is a blessing for me to pronounce them "husband and wife."

_____ (groom) and _____ (bride), please kneel and receive your parents' blessings on your marriage. Congregation, let us unite in silent prayer, asking for God's richest blessings to be poured out on this couple and their life together.

(The bride and groom will kneel, facing each other, as both sets of parents come to them, lay hands on them, and quietly offer their blessings on them. When the parents have prayed, the parents will return to their seats.)

(A soloist should sing a song, such as "Household of Faith," or a hymn, such as "Count Your Blessings," during the time of family blessing. The minister will conclude the time of family blessing with the benediction:)

"The LORD bless you and keep you; the LORD make his face shine upon you and be gracious to you; the LORD turn his face toward you and give you peace" (Num. 6:24–26), now and always. Amen.

(The bride and groom will stand and face the minister at the conclusion of the benediction.)

THE MARRIAGE PRONOUNCEMENT

This has truly been a blessed event! It is with joy and thanksgiving that I introduce to you Mr. and Mrs. _____. Go now with our blessing resting upon you.

THE RECESSIONAL

A Covenant Marriage

A Covenantal Wedding Ceremony

———— ❧ ————

THE PRELUDE

(Vocal and organ solos.)

THE CHIMING OF THE HOUR

THE SEATING OF THE GRANDMOTHERS

THE SOLO

(Song to be sung as the grandmothers are seated.)

THE SEATING OF THE MOTHERS

(Song to be sung as the mothers are seated.)

THE CANDLE LIGHTING

(Candles to be lit as the mothers are seated.)

THE PROCESSIONAL

THE WELCOME

Today we are all blessed to be joined as family and friends in witnessing the marriage of _____ (groom) and _____ (bride). While this is a joyous event to be celebrated and remembered for years to come, it is also a solemn event to be contemplated and honored with deep reverence for the lifetime commitment that these two make. It is with great love for each other and for God that _____ (groom) and _____ (bride) come today seeking to be united as one. Let us pray.

THE INVOCATION

O Lord, you are our beloved and most gracious Father. As our heavenly Parent and as the One in whose image we are made, you know well the emotions we are experiencing as we stand before your marriage altar. We are excited and yet nervous, hopeful and yet somewhat uncertain about this most sacred event in the lives of _____ (groom) and _____ (bride). As perhaps never before, we desire to feel your assuring and confirming presence with us in this hour. You have wonderfully made us to love and to unite with one special person whom you have made to be our complement, our life mate. As your children, we desire to share these life-changing moments with you and to sense your pleasure in the marriage of these two who dearly love you. Thank you for loving us and being with us today. For it is in the name of our Elder Brother, Jesus Christ, that we pray. Amen.

(The bride and groom should immediately join hands at the close of this prayer, as the bride's father steps back to meet the bride's mother, with both parents now standing next to each other at their seats.)

THE GIVING OF THE BRIDE

Who gives this bride in marriage?

Father and mother respond: "In love, we do."

(The father and mother of the bride sit following their response.)

THE SONG OF ASCENT

(Bride and groom walk up steps from the floor to the platform level as the song begins.)

THE STATEMENT OF MARRIAGE

What images are conjured up in your mind when you hear the word *marriage*? You probably picture loved ones or friends who are married—perhaps your parents. You may envision the two of you. How did God see marriage when he created it for mankind? We may look to God's Word to answer that question.

In the Bible, marriage is seen as an institution. Marriage is understood as instituted by God. It was his design and plan for the human race. In creation, God declared, "It is not good for the man to be alone. I will make a helper suitable for him" (Gen. 2:18). It was God who brought Eve to Adam after creating her, (Gen. 2:22), in effect pronouncing the first marriage union. In the New Testament, husband and wife are said to be "joined together" by God (Matt. 19:6). Jesus sanctioned marriage by his attendance at the marriage in Cana in Galilee (John 2:1–11).[1] Marriage may, thus, be seen by us as a God-given institution created and blessed for our benefit.

In the Bible, marriage is seen as a vocation. Men and women are called of God to be husbands and wives. Adam and Eve were given the "job description" for the vocation of marriage in the creation mandate: "Be fruitful and increase in number; fill the earth and subdue it. Rule over . . . every living creature" (Gen. 1:28). Today we understand the vocation of marriage calling for spouses to meet each other's needs for companionship and support, for spouses to join in procreation of offspring, for spouses to assume the parenting and nurturing roles for their offspring, and for spouses to provide for the physical needs of life and family.

In the Bible, marriage is seen as a covenant. Besides the institutional and vocational views of marriage, marriage is also viewed as a covenant

(Mal. 2:14). As a holy covenant made with God, Christian marriage implies a freely chosen, lifelong, exclusive relationship between the husband and wife under the authority of God. A covenant is the most solemn binding agreement into which two parties can enter. Marriage is not contractual but rather covenantal. It is important to note the difference between a covenant and a contract. A covenant is based on trust between parties; a contract is based on distrust. A covenant is based on unlimited responsibility; a contract is based on limited liability. A covenant cannot be broken if new circumstances occur; a contract can be voided by mutual consent.[2]

It is the covenantal view of marriage on which we will primarily focus. While the Bible's imagery of covenant focuses primarily on the covenants between God and humankind, there are biblical examples of covenants made between individuals. One of the most touching examples of such a covenant is found in 1 Samuel: "Jonathan made a covenant with David because he loved him as himself. Jonathan took off the robe he was wearing and gave it to David, along with his tunic, and even his sword, his bow and his belt" (1 Sam. 18:3–4). The giving of these items was the sign or seal of the trustworthiness of this covenant. There are parallels in this covenant between friends who loved each other as brothers and the covenant of marriage between a husband and wife.

In covenant making, the *exchanging of robes* was a way of committing everything one had—including oneself and one's possessions—to the other. It signified two becoming one. It was like taking on the identity of—or exchanging names with—the other person. In marriage we commit everything to our marriage partner. We share all of ourselves and all of our possessions without reserve. We also exchange names—with wives most frequently taking on the surname of their husbands.

In covenant making, the *giving of weapons* symbolized the covenantal partners' responsibility to defend the other from his enemies. Covenantal partners were responsible for the protection of each other. In marriage we assume the responsibility for the well-being of our mate. We pledge to stand by him or her, no matter life's circumstances. We commit ourselves to his or her protection and defense in adversity.

In covenant making, the *giving of the belt* was symbolic of the giving of one's strength for the well-being of his covenantal partner. The belt was the part of the armor that held the weapons. As such, it became the symbol of man's strength. In marriage, we commit our strength to "holding up" our partner and carrying the weight of our partner's burdens. We pledge always to be there for him or her in unwavering support. In doing so, we provide our mate with a reservoir of strength and confidence, encouragement and trust.

How strong is the bond of the marriage covenant? The marital bond is to be one of total commitment, complete faithfulness, and permanence. Established and blessed by God, the marriage covenant is not to be broken. It is to be honored among all people. _____ (groom) and _____ (bride), today you must leave your parents and cleave to the spouse God has given you. With your new spouse you will experience the strongest of all human bonds—the covenant of marriage.

THE VOWS

_____ (groom) and _____ (bride), are you ready now to be joined in this covenant of marriage?

Groom and bride respond: "We are."

_____ (groom), will you have _____ (bride) to be your wife, and live together with her in holy marriage? Will you love her, comfort her, honor her, respect her, and keep her? Will you forsake all others and be faithful to her as long as you both shall live?

Groom responds: "I will."

_____ (bride), will you have _____ (groom) to be your husband, and live together with him in holy marriage? Will you love him, comfort him, honor him, respect him, and keep him? Will you forsake all others and be faithful to him as long as you both shall live?

Bride responds: "I will."

_____ (groom) and _____ (bride), will you face each other and repeat these covenantal vows after me?

Groom: "I, _____ (groom), enter into this covenant of marriage with you, _____ (bride). I promise always to love you as my wife and to completely give myself and all that I have to you. I pledge to care for you in sickness or in health. I will honor and cherish you all the days of my life, whether our life circumstances are better or worse, richer or poorer. I will strive to live before you a life of faith and trust in Jesus Christ."

Bride: "I, _____ (bride), enter into this covenant of marriage with you, _____ (groom). I promise always to love you as my husband and to completely give myself and all that I have to you. I pledge to care for you in sickness or in health. I will honor and cherish you all the days of my life, whether our life circumstances are better or worse, richer or poorer. I will strive to live before you a life of faith and trust in Jesus Christ."

THE RINGS

In your covenant relationship, the rings which you are about to exchange symbolize your commitment to honoring the terms of the marriage covenant. As symbols, your rings, thereby, serve as visual reminders to all of the vows you made.

_____ (groom), will you take the ring and place it on _____'s (bride's) finger? Repeat after me:

Groom: "I give you this ring as a symbol of my commitment to you and, thereby, seal this covenant of marriage."

_____ (bride), will you take the ring and place it on _____'s (groom's) finger? Repeat after me:

Bride: "I give you this ring as a symbol of my commitment to you and, thereby, seal this covenant of marriage."

THE PRONOUNCEMENT

_____ (groom) and _____ (bride), you have exchanged the solemn covenantal vows of marriage and have given rings as the sign and seal of your covenant. By the authority vested in me as a minister of the gospel and by the state of _____, I joyfully pronounce that you are husband and wife.

You have requested that your first act together as husband and wife not be the usual wedding kiss—although that will soon come; rather, that your first act as husband and wife be one of faith and obedience to the One who gave his life for you and made valid his covenant with you—your Lord and Savior, Jesus Christ. Will you kneel to partake of the Lord's Supper as your family and friends bow in prayer for your marriage?

THE LORD'S SUPPER

Jesus Christ established a new covenant, the covenant of grace, and enters into this covenant with those who embrace him as their personal Lord and Savior. At the last supper Jesus shared with his disciples, he "took bread, gave thanks and broke it, and gave it to his disciples, saying, 'Take and eat; this is my body.' Then he took the cup, gave thanks and offered it to them, saying, 'Drink from it, all of you. This is my blood of the covenant, which is poured out for many for the forgiveness of sins'" (Matt. 26:26–28). _____ (groom) and _____ (bride), as you observe the Lord's Supper, you will partake of the most precious symbols of the new covenant: the broken body and spilled blood of Jesus Christ. You will also identify with the One who died to save you from sin.

In the second chapter of Galatians we read, "I have been crucified with Christ and I no longer live, but Christ lives in me. The life I live in the body, I live by faith in the Son of God, who loved me and gave himself for me" (Gal. 2:20). _____ (groom) and _____ (bride), as you assume your new identity as husband and wife, you will also always keep your identity with the Son who loved us and gave himself for us. As you assume the name, "Mr. and Mrs. _____ *(groom's full name)*," you will also proudly and humbly keep the name, *Christian,* which will forever identify you with the One who shed his blood for you.

THE SONG AND PRAYER OF CONSECRATION

(The groom and bride will kneel on the kneeling bench as the song begins. They will remain in this posture as they partake of the Lord's Supper and throughout the song and the prayer of consecration. The minister will quietly administer the Lord's Supper to the couple. Following the administration of the elements and a time of silent prayer as the song is sung, the minister will pray:)

Sovereign Father, we recognize that it was never necessary for you to condescend to making any covenant with man. In a display of unparalleled love and mercy, however, you chose to draw us closer to you through your gracious covenants with man. Thank you for what you have done for us in redemptive history. Thank you, also, for what you have done today. In your providential care, you have brought _____ (groom) and _____ (bride) together in a loving relationship and, now, in marriage. We praise you for perfectly modeling covenantal relations so that these two may know how to proceed in honoring the vows they have made today. We ask your guidance and blessings for _____ (groom) and _____ (bride) as they seek to follow your example of love and faithfulness. In the name of the Covenant Maker, Jesus Christ, we pray. Amen.

(The bride and groom will stand at the conclusion of the prayer.)

_____ (groom), you may now kiss your bride.

THE SIGNING OF THE COVENANT OF MARRIAGE

_____ (groom) and _____ (bride), you may now sign "The Covenant of Marriage."

(The couple will stop briefly to sign "The Covenant of Marriage" before recessing. Following the recessional, others in the wedding party may sign the covenant agreement.)

THE RECESSIONAL

THE POSTLUDE

The Perfect Garden Wedding

A Ceremony for an Outdoor Wedding
(This ceremony can be easily modified for weddings held inside.)

THE HYMNS OF PRELUDE

(Alternate the singing of hymns—by the congregation or by the singers—with the reading of Scripture. The use of wind instruments [e.g., flute or clarinet] and the use of stringed instruments [e.g., guitar or violin] would greatly complement the setting.)

"In the beginning God created the heavens and the earth" (Gen. 1:1).

This Is My Father's World

"God saw all that he had made, and it was very good" (Gen. 1:31).

I Sing the Mighty Power of God

"Giving thanks always for all things unto God" (Eph. 5:20 KJV).

For the Beauty of the Earth

"There is none like unto . . . God" (Deut. 33:26 KJV).

How Great Thou Art

"I will awaken the dawn, I will praise you, O Lord" (Ps. 57:8–9).

Morning Has Broken

"My lips shall . . . rejoice when I sing unto thee" (Ps. 71:23 KJV).

Joyful, Joyful, We Adore Thee

THE SEATING OF THE GRANDMOTHERS

"I was young and now I am old, yet I have never seen the righteous forsaken or their children begging bread. They are always generous and lend freely; their children will be blessed . . . For the LORD loves the just and will not forsake his faithful ones" (Ps. 37:25–26, 28).

Great Is Thy Faithfulness

THE SEATING OF THE MOTHERS

"These are the commands, decrees and laws the LORD your God directed me to teach you to observe . . . so that you, your children and their children after them may fear the LORD your God as long as you live by keeping all his decrees and commands that I give you, and so that you may enjoy long life. The LORD our God, the LORD is one. Love the LORD your God with all your heart and with all your soul and with all your strength. These commandments that I give you today are to be upon your hearts. Impress them on your children. Talk about them when you sit at home and when you walk along the road, when you lie down and when you get up" (Deut. 6:1–2, 4–7).

My Tribute

THE PROCESSIONAL

(The father of the bride gives his daughter's hand to the groom. He is then seated with the mother.)

THE WELCOME

_____ (groom) and _____ (bride) would like to welcome you, their beloved family and dear friends. Since childhood, they have thought about what their future wedding day would be like. As they fell in love and were drawn to marriage, they dreamed about what would make theirs the perfect wedding. They decided that the glory of God's creation, as we now experience it in this beautiful outdoor setting, would be the perfect backdrop to this time of worship, celebration, and commitment. The hymns they have chosen reflect the glory of God and the wonders of his created order. As God alone is perfect, let us now worship him in the singing of a hymn, *Praise to the Lord, the Almighty.* Please stand for the singing of this hymn of praise.

THE HYMN OF PRAISE

> *Praise to the Lord, the Almighty*

(This hymn is to be sung by the congregation. They are to stand for the hymn and then be seated for its conclusion.)

THE INVOCATION

O Lord, you alone are perfect in all your being, and you alone deserve all of our worship and adoration. You are like the morning sun: warming us with your presence, sustaining us with your gracious benefit, and radiating your light and love in all who would reflect your character. We see the splendor of these surroundings and we are drawn to reflect upon the glory of your creation. We hear the sounds of nature and anticipate the day in which the rocks will cry out in praise of you. As we think on these things, our hearts are stirred with emotions of gratitude and adoration. Thank you for this glorious day of days. As you bless us with your presence, help us to understand just what makes a wedding perfect. We offer now our praise and devotion to you. In your name only we pray. Amen.

THE WEDDING CHARGE

_____ (groom) and _____ (bride) seek the perfect wedding. What is the perfect wedding? In all honesty, I believe that there was only one perfect earthly wedding. You have said that you both dreamed of the perfect wedding. Well, let me tell you that God, too, dreamed of the perfect wedding. He could have held it any place, but, like you, he chose an outdoor setting for his perfect wedding. There, at creation, in the Garden of Eden, God united Adam and Eve as husband and wife. The flowers were perfect in this incredible paradise on earth which provided the perfect setting in which this perfect couple was wed. The music was perfect as the creatures lifted their voices in perfect harmony. The bride and groom were perfectly attired—yes, attired— being clothed in righteousness.

We read in Scripture that even the wedding gifts were perfect. As his perfect gift, God gave them authority over all creation. "'Subdue [the earth]. Rule over the fish of the sea and the birds of the air and over every living creature that moves on the ground.' Then God said, 'I give you every seed-bearing plant on the face of the whole earth and every tree that has fruit with seed in it. They will be yours'" (Gen. 1:28*b*–29). It was a wedding to be remembered and to serve as an example to all others. It was a glorious and perfect wedding day on earth.

So, then, what has changed? Can you not hope for a perfect wedding? My answer to you would first be "no," and then be "yes." Let me explain. Since the time of that first perfect wedding, there has come the advent of sin. With the Fall of Man, our relationship to God and to one another has changed. Sin has caused us to desire that which is not purely perfect—oftentimes, far from it. Our desires pale in comparison to the righteousness of God. Our priorities are often not those of our heavenly Father. From the time of Adam and Eve's wedding, there have only been mere shadows of perfection in weddings that have followed.

Are shadows necessarily bad? Of course not. In fact, we can strive to emulate the character and example of Christ—in our lives, in our weddings, and in our marriages. In doing so, we are then more free to turn all of life's plans, hopes, and dreams over to him in submission to his perfect will.

- We can seek his guidance for the perfect—or almost perfect— mate. This you both have done.

- We can offer him our lives—apart and together—for service to him and for the accomplishment of his kingdom work on earth. This you both have done.

- We can keep ourselves pure and allow the Holy Spirit to dwell richly in us. This is evidenced as to what you both have done.

- We can vow to establish a family of faith that will be a home which evidences the joy and love of the Lord as well as the love and appreciation for each family member. This, too, is what you both intend to do.

_____ (groom) and _____ (bride), while you cannot know an absolutely perfect wedding or marriage in your lifetime on earth, you can strive for a really good shadow of that perfection!

Well, if the answer to our having the perfect wedding on earth is "no," why, then, did I say "yes" to our hoping for a perfect wedding? All of these weddings, from that of Adam and Eve to those earthly shadows which followed, point to the consummate and absolutely perfect wedding, the wedding of the Lamb of God. We can visualize what this perfect wedding will be like through reading its description from the words of the Groom-to-Be himself, Jesus Christ, as given to John and recorded in the nineteenth chapter of Revelation: "'Hallelujah! For our Lord God Almighty reigns. Let us rejoice and be glad and give him glory! For the wedding of the Lamb has come, and his bride has made herself ready. Fine linen, bright and clean, was given her to wear.' [Fine linen stands for the righteous acts of the saints.] Then the angel said to me, 'Write: "Blessed are those who are invited to the wedding supper of the Lamb!"' And he added, 'These are the true words of God'" (Rev. 19:6*b*–9).

When Christ returns for his bride, the church, only then, at the marriage feast of the Lamb, can we know—in whole—heavenly perfection in a wedding. From the perfect clothing of righteousness to the perfect wedding setting of the new paradise to the perfect mate for all eternity, you, _____ (groom) and _____ (bride), as believers and followers of Jesus Christ, can hope for *and* experience the perfect wedding.

As we approach this sacred time of making your wedding vows and of exchanging symbols of that commitment, it is my duty to ask: _____ (groom) and _____ (bride), are you ready to commit your lives to striving to love each other and God as Christ perfectly loved his bride, the church?

Groom and bride respond: "We are."

THE VOWS AND RING CEREMONY

_____ (groom), do you take _____ (bride) to be your wife? Do you make a vow before God and in the presence of these witnesses that you will love her, honor her, cherish her in all of life's circumstances, as you both seek to serve the Lord, as long as you both shall live?

Groom responds: "I do."

_____ (bride), do you take _____ (groom) to be your husband? Do you make a vow before God and in the presence of these witnesses that you will love him, honor him, cherish him in all of life's circumstances, as you both seek to serve the Lord, as long as you both shall live?

Bride responds: "I do."

_____ (groom) and _____ (bride) have chosen to continue making their vows as they give each other their wedding rings. May I have the rings?

(At this point, the best man and the maid or matron of honor give the minister the rings by placing them on his Bible. The bride and groom face each other. They will each say their vows, take their rings from the

minister's Bible, and give their rings to each other without the prompting of the minister. Of course, the prompting by the minister as they exchange vows and rings is an option.)

Groom: "_____ (bride), I cannot imagine a more perfect mate than you, except for our perfect Lord and Savior. I know you are the woman for whom I have prayed to be my wife, my partner, my companion, and my best friend. You alone are the one with whom I want to serve God, to establish a home, and to raise a godly family. I promise I will cherish you, love you, pray for you, and never forsake you all the days of my life. With God's help, I will strive always to treat you in a Christlike manner. *(The groom takes the ring from the minister's Bible and places it on the bride's finger.)* I give you this ring as a sign and seal of my unconditional love for you and of my covenant with you and with God. May he make us one in him."

Bride: "_____ (groom), I cannot imagine a more perfect mate than you, except for our perfect Lord and Savior. I know you are the man for whom I have prayed to be my husband, my partner, my companion, and my best friend. You alone are the one with whom I want to serve God, to establish a home, and to raise a godly family. I promise I will cherish you, love you, pray for you, and never forsake you all the days of my life. With God's help, I will strive always to treat you in a Christlike manner. *(The bride takes the ring from the minister's Bible and places it on the groom's finger.)* I give you this ring as a sign and seal of my unconditional love for you and of my covenant with you and with God. May he make us one in him."

THE TIME OF PRAYER

(The couple kneels for time of prayer.)

Let us pray.

(There is first a time of silent prayer while a solo, O Perfect Love, *is sung. The minister will pray following the solo:)*

Creator of all that is perfect, we praise you for this "nearly perfect" wedding day and for union of _____ (groom) and _____ (bride) in marriage. We pray that you will bless their lives together as husband and wife, their service to you, and in the establishment of their home and family. We pray that you will keep them ever in your loving care until the time they are to behold you in all your perfection. In the name of the Father, and of the Son, and of the Holy Spirit. Amen.

THE PRONOUNCEMENT

_____ (groom) and _____ (bride), you have made your solemn vows and have exchanged symbols of your love. With confidence that God will bless your union, it is my distinct privilege to pronounce you husband and wife. _____ (groom), you may kiss your bride.

(The bride receives her floral bouquet from her attendant. The couple turns and faces those present.)

It is my honor to present to you Mr. and Mrs. _____.

THE RECESSIONAL

THE POSTLUDE OF PRAISE

(The instrumentalists will conclude the service by playing joyful hymns of praise as the guests depart.)

The Ideal Christmas Gift

A Ceremony for a Christmas Wedding

THE PRELUDE OF CAROLS

(Alternate the singing of hymns—by the congregation or by the singers—with the reading of Scripture. The use of handbells or brass instruments would greatly aid this time of worship.)

"The angel said, '. . . I bring you good news of great joy'" (Luke 2:10).

Angels, from the Realms of Glory

"The promise which was made . . . God hath fulfilled" (Acts 13:32–33 KJV).

Come, Thou Long-Expected Jesus

"A great company . . . appeared with the angel . . . saying, 'Glory to God in the highest'" (Luke 2:13–14).

Angels We Have Heard on High

"'They will call him Immanuel'—which means, 'God with us'" (Matt. 1:23).

> *Emmanuel*

"With joy shall ye draw water out of the wells of salvation" (Isa. 12:3 KJV).

> *How Great Our Joy*

THE SOLO AND THE LIGHTING OF THE CANDLES

(The mothers are escorted down the aisle to the front of the church, where they light the candles. They are then escorted to their seats.)

"But when the time had fully come, God sent his Son, born of a woman, born under law, to redeem those under law, that we might receive full rights of sons" (Gal. 4:4–5). "And [Mary] brought forth her firstborn son, and wrapped him in swaddling clothes, and laid him in a manger" (Luke 2:7 KJV).

> *Love Came Down at Christmas*

THE CHIMING OF THE HOUR

THE PROCESSIONAL

THE WELCOME

Welcome! What a joyous day this is for _____ (groom) and _____ (bride) and for all of us who love them! What an incredible time of year they have chosen as their wedding date! This is the season which celebrates God's love being made manifest in the birth of his Son, Jesus Christ. This is the season that is characterized by gift giving to our loved ones. We are here today to celebrate God's love as demonstrated in the life of his Son and in the lives of _____ (groom) and _____ (bride). We are here today to recognize that marriage is a gift given by God to demonstrate his love for us as he seeks to fulfill us, as individuals and as a couple, and to conform us, as maturing believers, into the image of Christ.

THE CONGREGATIONAL CALL TO PRAISE

Congregation of witnesses, please stand and join me in reading responsively the Call to Praise of our Lord and Savior, followed by the singing of a carol.

Pastor: O come, let us adore him!

Congregation: O come, let us adore him!

Pastor: "For to us a child is born,

Congregation: To us a son is given,

Pastor: And the government will be on his shoulders.

Congregation: And he will be called Wonderful Counselor,

Pastor: Mighty God,

Congregation: Everlasting Father,

Pastor: Prince of Peace.

Congregation: Of the increase of his government and peace

Pastor: There will be no end" (Isa. 9:6–7*a*).

Congregation: O come, let us adore him!

Pastor: O come, let us adore him!

ALL: O come, let us adore him, Christ the Lord!

THE CONGREGATIONAL CAROL

O Come, All Ye Faithful

THE INVOCATION

Let us pray. O holy Child of Bethlehem, the reigning King of glory, Lord of heaven and earth, we come in your name, the name that is above every other name, before whom all knees shall bow and every tongue confess that you alone are Lord. With hearts that are humble, we come into your divine presence. With hearts full of gratitude, we thank you for coming to earth as a human baby, God's ideal Christmas gift for mankind. As you now condescend to hear our prayers, we are mindful of your grace and are ever grateful to be in your presence. For in your presence is the gift of life; in your presence is the gift of love.

We join with you and the heavenly hosts to witness this marriage, as _____ (groom) and _____ (bride) commit their lives to you and to each other, and receive your ideal Christmas gift for them, the gift of Christian marriage. Bless them as they unwrap this gift in the days and years to come. In the powerful name of our Messiah, God with us, Immanuel. Amen.

THE DECLARATION OF INTENT

_____ (groom), do you believe it to be the will of God for you to receive _____ (bride) as his ideal gift for your life and as your wife in Christian marriage?

Groom responds: "I do."

Are you ready to promise to her and to our Lord that you will keep the vows that you speak today?

Groom responds: "I am."

_____ (bride), do you believe it to be the will of God for you to receive _____ (groom) as his ideal gift for your life and as your husband in Christian marriage?

Bride responds: "I do."

Are you ready to promise to him and to our Lord that you will keep the vows you speak today?

Bride responds: "I am."

THE GIVING OF THE BRIDE

Who gives _____ (bride) to be married to _____ (groom) in good faith that promises to be made today at this altar (*or* "place") will be kept?

Father responds: "I do."

THE MEDITATION ON MARRIAGE

Do you ever struggle with selecting the ideal Christmas gift for someone you love? We all have. Sometimes our choices seem to be inspired. Sometimes our choices are only a day away from being the cause of the recipient's waiting in the long "returns" line at the local department store. We read that some gift givers employ the services of a professional shopper for ease in gift selection and purchase. While there are extenuating circumstances where people might not be able to do their own shopping, most of us acknowledge that the better way to select and give a gift—especially for a loved one—is through paying attention to the needs of the loved one receiving the gift, carefully selecting the ideal gift that will meet those needs, and sacrificially giving of one's resources to purchase that ideal gift for our loved one.

God is the master gift giver. We can look to him to be our heavenly example of the best way to choose and give ideal gifts to our loved ones.

God was aware of the gift needs of his loved ones. Mankind was lost and in need of a Savior. Without a Savior, they were unable to live in righteous obedience to God's Law. We read in the Epistle to the Romans: "For all have sinned and fall short of the glory of God" (Rom. 3:23 NASB). This epistle goes on to say that mankind was in need of One who could save them from the penalty of their sin: "For the wages of sin is death" (Rom. 6:23a NASB). Mankind would receive the death sentence without a stay of execution. The penalty imposed for mankind's sin was eternal punishment and separation from God. God, as the just judge of mankind, was well aware of the needs of those he loved.

God carefully selected the ideal gift that could satisfy the needs of his loved ones. We read in the Book of James that God was the consummate Christmas shopper: "Every good and perfect gift is from above, coming down from the Father of the heavenly lights" (Jas. 1:17). God, in his infinite wisdom, selected and gave only the good and perfect gift that could meet the needs of his loved one. You know the verse: "For God so loved the world, that he gave his only begotten Son" (John 3:16*a*, KJV). But do you remember why God selected his only Son to be his ideal gift to mankind? Recall now all of the verse, all of John 3:16, KJV: "For God so loved the world, that he gave his only begotten Son, that whosoever believeth in him should not perish, but have everlasting life." God's gift of his Son has some parallels to our giving a gift certificate that may be redeemed to purchase what we need. God gave the world his only Son so that the price may be satisfied through redemption that we might receive the gift of eternal life in his divine presence and as his adopted children.

God sacrificially gave of himself to purchase the ideal Christmas gift for his loved ones. We may be a little confused about the cost of God's gift when we read all of Romans 6:23 (NASB): "For the wages of sin is death, but the free gift of God is eternal life in Christ Jesus our Lord." Do not be mistaken. God was not a cheapskate. While the language of this verse might cause some confusion, there is no confusion in Scripture concerning the great price God paid to purchase this gift for his loved ones. *"You have been redeemed, at tremendous cost"* (1 Cor. 7:23*a* PHILLIPS). God gave of himself sacrificially to purchase the ideal Christmas gift for us, so we might be made holy and blameless. In his Word we are told: "We have been made holy through the sacrifice of the body of Jesus Christ once for all" (Heb. 10:10). "Greater love has no one than this, that he lay down his life for his friends" (John 15:13). The greatest price of all—the very life of the Son of God—was paid to show God's love through the purchase of this ideal Christmas gift.

Are you a good gift giver? You are called to be one in marriage. And it is more than remembering birthdays and anniversaries, holidays and special occasions—although that helps! In Scripture, you are instructed to give the gift of yourself—wholly and completely—to this one that you love and to whom you are about to be married. "Husbands, love your wives, just as Christ loved the church and gave himself up for her" (Eph. 5:25). _____ (bride), you are not off the hook. Early in that same chapter of Ephesians, you will find instructions to you: "Be imitators of God,

. . . and live a life of love, just as Christ loved us and gave himself up for us as a fragrant offering and sacrifice to God" (5:1–2).

What price are you willing to pay in order to give this most cherished loved one the ideal Christmas gift? As believers in Jesus Christ and recipients of God's gracious gift of salvation, how will you respond in love to this one by whom you stand? Will your Christmas wedding always be remembered as the day when each of you began unwrapping the wonderful gift of Christian marriage and as the first day of many to come in which you followed God's example of sacrificial giving to this one that you love? When you say, "Merry Christmas" to each other in the Christmases to come, will you remember this day and be conveying with these two words that you love each other with the sacrificial love of God and desire to give each other only God's ideal gift?

If this reflects your heart's desire, look now into the eyes of this one who stands beside you, and repeat together after me:

Groom and bride: "Following Christ's example of love, I stand ready to give myself sacrificially to you in marriage."

THE EXCHANGE OF VOWS AND RINGS

_____ (groom) and _____ (bride), would you face each other, join your hands in love, and repeat after me?

Groom: "I, _____ (groom), give myself—totally and completely—to you in Christian marriage. I will seek to follow God's example of sacrificial giving. I promise that I will love, honor, and cherish you all the days of my life. I will seek the best for your life as we grow in our love for each other and for God and as we seek to honor him in our union. It is with joy and gratitude that I receive you, _____ (bride), as God's ideal gift as my mate in Christian marriage, just as I received Christ as my Savior."

Bride: "I, _____ (bride), give myself—totally and completely—to you in Christian marriage. I will seek to follow God's example of sacrificial giving. I promise that I will love, honor, and cherish you all the days of my life. I will seek the best for your life as we grow in our love for each other and for God and as we seek to honor him in our union. It is with joy and gratitude that I receive you, _____ (groom), as God's ideal gift as my mate in Christian marriage, just as I received Christ as my Savior."

_____ (groom), as you hold the hand of _____ (bride), place this ring on her finger and repeat these words of commitment:

Groom: "I, _____ (groom), give this ring to you, _____ (bride), as a seal of the vows I have made to you and to God. May it always symbolize the gift of our love and of God's love for us."

Bride: "I, _____ (bride), give this ring to you, _____ (groom), as a seal of the vows I have made to you and to God. May it always symbolize the gift of our love and of God's love for us."

THE SONG OF CONSECRATION

(The couple will kneel in prayer as the song begins.)

O Little Town of Bethlehem (stanza 4) "O holy Child of Bethlehem, descend to us we pray. Cast out our sin, and enter in; be born in us today! We hear the Christmas angels the great glad tidings tell. O come to us, abide in us, our Lord Immanuel!"

THE BENEDICTION

Savior of mankind, thank you for the demonstration of your love in the lives of these your servants, _____ (groom) and _____ (bride). Bless their union. Bless their relationship to each other and to you. And now, Father, give your benediction. May your grace, love, and peace abide now and forever with _____ (groom) and _____ (bride). May your heavenly favor rest upon them. May you open their eyes even more fully to the gift of your love. In Jesus' name we pray. Amen.

(The couple will rise and face the minister.)

THE PRONOUNCEMENT

_____ (groom) and _____ (bride), by the authority granted me by the laws of this state and as a minister of the gospel of Christ, I pronounce you are husband and wife, Mr. and Mrs. _____ (groom's full name), to the glory of God.

THE RECESSIONAL

Angels We Have Heard on High

THE CAROLS OF POSTLUDE

Carol of the Bells

I Heard the Bells on Christmas Day

The Birthday of a King (refrain)

Blended Lives

**A Ceremony for Second Marriages with
Optional Vows for Children**

THE WELCOME

We come together for the purpose of affirming the leadership of the Lord in bringing _____ (groom) and _____ (bride) to this significant moment in their lives. They have desired that you join them as witnesses and encouragers. Your prayers, counsel, and friendship have given them strength and hope. For that they are grateful.

THE INVOCATION

Let us join in prayer, asking God to bless us today: King of glory, you have made us for your glory. You alone are glorious. Your glory is our joy. We pray that your glory may be seen in this service of commitment and experienced in the lives of _____ (groom), _____ (bride), and all those present in this sacred hour. To your everlasting glory we lift our praise and thanksgiving. Amen.

THE STATEMENT OF MARRIAGE

We know that it is God's will for marriage to last a lifetime. We also know, however, that from the very beginning, Satan has attacked God's supreme creation by waging war against the first institution, the home and the family. He has sought to corrupt marriage by every divisive means possible, from death to unfaithfulness, immorality to abandonment, abuse to neglect. These painful situations have brought division and destruction to marriages and to family units.

We know that as followers of Jesus Christ, we are called to follow a different standard than that of the world. Our responsibility is to live as salt and light in a world of decay and darkness. We find God's standard for marriage reflected in Paul's letter to the Ephesians: "We are part of his body. And this is why a man leaves father and mother and cherishes his wife. No longer two, they become 'one flesh'" (Eph. 5:30–31, TMNT). By God's command, marriage is sacred. Marriage is important.

_____ (groom) and _____ (bride) have experienced circumstances not of their own choosing. They have sought God's will as they have worked through their broken relationships and past experiences. They believe that God has led them to each other. They have found—and are finding—forgiveness, healing, and grace as they walk this journey of faith and unconditional love with God and with each other. They believe that their desire to be united in marriage has been confirmed by God and does not violate the truths of his Word.

As they blend their lives (*if applicable, add:* "and families"), they desire to establish a home that will be God-led, God-blessed, and God-glorifying. As they share their vows today, they humble themselves before a gracious God and ask his blessing on their marriage. (*If applicable, add this sentence:* "It is important to _____ (groom) and _____ (bride) that their children have stability, security, and significance in their home. They ask that their children join them in the making of vows and in the blending of these two homes.")

THE GIVING OF THE BRIDE (OPTIONAL)

Believing that _____ (groom) and _____ (bride) are committed to building a marriage bridge that will endure, it is my honor to ask, "Who gives this bride to be married to this man?"

(If applicable) *Children respond:* "We do."

THE VOWS

_____ (groom), face _____ (bride) and repeat after me: "I, _____ (groom), take you, _____ (bride), to be my wife for the rest of my life. I promise God and I promise you that I will not dishonor his name or your trust. I will love you as Christ loves the church. I will earnestly seek God's will for our family. I will allow God's Spirit to fill me and produce in me the character of Christ. I will make you, above all others, my first priority. I will be devoted to you and will reserve my affections for you alone. *(If children are involved, this sentence could be added for both parties:* "I will work with you to teach our children to know, love, and obey you, and will stand by you in giving guidance and leadership.") I will make it my highest goal to bring glory to God through my life and through the oneness of our lives together. I make these vows in the name of our glorious Savior. Amen."

_____ (bride), face _____ (groom) and repeat after me: "I, _____ (bride), take you, _____ (groom), to be my husband for the rest of my life. I promise God and I promise you that I will not dishonor his name or your trust. I will honor and respect you as God made you. I will earnestly seek God's will for our family. I will allow God's Spirit to fill me and produce in me the character of Christ. I will make you, above all others, my first priority. I will be devoted to you and will reserve my affections for you alone. *(If children are involved, this sentence could be added for both parties:* "I will work with you to teach our children to know, love, and obey you, and will stand by you in giving guidance and leadership.") I will make it my highest goal to bring glory to God through my life and through the oneness of our lives together. I make these vows in the name of our glorious Savior. Amen."

THE RING CEREMONY

_____ (groom), will you place the ring on _____'s (bride's) finger and repeat after me:

Groom: "With gladness and promise, I give you this ring, as a witness of my vows to you and my pledge to keep them. In the name of the God of all grace, who has saved us and keeps us. Amen."

_____ (bride), will you place the ring on _____'s (groom's) finger and repeat after me:

Bride: "With gladness and promise, I give you this ring, as a witness of my vows to you and my pledge to keep them. In the name of the God of all grace, who has saved us and keeps us. Amen."

THE VOWS MADE WITH CHILDREN BY A PREVIOUS MARRIAGE

(The following vows[1] are optional and are for weddings that involve a child or children from a previous marriage.)

Today's wedding is unique in that we are including _____ (children's names) in the vows. It's not unique in the sense that people with children get married. It is unique, because _____ (groom) and _____ (bride) want it publicly known, and especially known to _____ (children's names), that this marriage includes _____ (him, her, or them). _____ (he, she, or they) is/are special. _____ (he, she, or they) is/are accepted. _____ (he, she, or they) is/are (a) vital, dynamic member(s) of this union today. With this in mind . . .

THE VOWS MADE WITH THE BRIDE'S CHILDREN BY A PREVIOUS MARRIAGE

Vows for the groom to pledge to the bride's children:

Do you, _____ (groom), promise to love _____ (children's names) as your own _____ (daughter, son, or children), according to God's purposes? Do you promise to treat _____ (her, him, or them) fairly, to be the best father possible with the wisdom that comes from our heavenly Father? Do you promise to administer justice in discipline, to be fair and supportive in trouble, and to respond with joy in _____ (her, his, or their) triumphs? Do you so promise?

Groom responds: "I do."

Vows for the children's mother, the bride, to pledge to her children:

Do you, _____ (bride), promise to love your _____ (daughter, son, or children) according to God's purposes? Do you promise not to allow prejudice toward _____ (her, him, or them) and _____ (her, his, or their) relationship to _____ (her, his, or their) loved ones to intrude into your marriage? Do you promise to treat _____ (her, him, or them) fairly in disagreements, and to support and strengthen this new family union? Do you promise to administer grace to your husband and _____ (daughter, son, or children), as you have received grace from our heavenly Father? Do you so promise?

Bride responds: "I do."

Vows for the bride's children:

_____, (children's names), do you promise to love your mother and her new husband? Do you promise to support their marriage and your new family? Do you promise to accept the responsibility of being their _____ (daughter, son, or children), and to encourage them, support them, and accept them just as our heavenly Father accepts us? Do you so promise?

Children respond: "I do," or "We do."

THE RING CEREMONY FOR THE BRIDE'S CHILDREN (OPTIONAL)

_____ (groom) is going to present a ring to _____ (children's names) on behalf of himself and _____ (bride's name). _____ (children's names), this ring is a token of remembrance. You are to remember that today, _____ (date), you were a witness to _____'s (groom's) and your mother's wedding vows. They also made vows to you, and you to them. This ring you will wear signifies their lasting love for you and their unending commitment to you.

_____ (groom), please place the ring on _____ (child's name) finger and repeat after me:

Groom: " _____ (child's name), I give you this ring as a token of your mother's love and of my love for you. It symbolizes our commitment to cherish you as an important part of our family and to always love and care for you."

(Repeat the ring vow for each child.)

THE VOWS MADE WITH THE GROOM'S CHILDREN BY A PREVIOUS MARRIAGE

Vows for the bride to pledge to the groom's children:

Do you, _____ (bride), promise to love _____ (children's names) as your own _____ (daughter, son, or children), according to God's purposes? Do you promise to treat _____ (her, him, or them) fairly, to be the best mother possible with the wisdom that comes from our heavenly Father? Do you promise to administer justice in discipline, to be fair and supportive in trouble, and to respond with joy in _____ (her, his, or their) triumphs? Do you so promise?

Bride responds: "I do."

Vows for the children's father, the groom, to pledge to his children:

Do you, _____ (groom), promise to love your _____ (daughter, son, or children) according to God's purposes? Do you promise not to allow prejudice toward _____ (her, him, or them) and _____ (her, his, or their) relationship to _____ (her, his, or their) loved ones to intrude into your marriage? Do you promise to treat _____ (her, him, or them) fairly in disagreements and to support and strengthen this new family union? Do you promise to administer grace to your wife and _____ (daughter, son, or children), as you have received grace from our heavenly Father? Do you so promise?

Groom responds: "I do."

Vows for the groom's children:

_____, (children's names), do you promise to love your father and his new wife? Do you promise to support their marriage and your new family? Do you promise to accept the responsibility of being their _____ (daughter, son, or children), and to encourage them, support them, and accept them just as our heavenly Father accepts us? Do you so promise?

Children respond: "I do," or "We do."

THE OPTIONAL RING CEREMONY FOR THE GROOM'S CHILDREN

_____ (bride) is going to present a ring to _____ (children's names) on behalf of herself and _____ (groom's name). _____ (children's names), this ring is a token of remembrance. You are to remember that today, _____ (date), you were a witness to _____'s (bride's) and your father's wedding vows. They also made vows to you, and you to them. This ring you will wear signifies their lasting love for you and their unending commitment to you.

_____ (bride), please place the ring on _____'s (child's name) finger and repeat after me:

Bride: " _____ (child's name), I give you this ring as a token of your father's love and of my love for you. It symbolizes our commitment to cherish you as an important part of our family and always to love and care for you."

(Repeat the ring vow for each child.)

THE PRONOUNCEMENT

_____ (groom) and _____ (bride), because of your promises made to God, [your children *(if applicable)*] and to each other, and because of your commitment to Christ and your dependence on his grace to empower you to keep these vows, I pronounce you are one in Christ until he receives you into his eternal home. Amen.

Broken and Restored

A Ceremony for Remarriage to a Former Mate

———— ✧ ————

THE PRELUDE

THE PROCESSIONAL

THE WELCOME

Family and friends, what a remarkable day this is! This is a celebration of what God has done and is doing in our midst. This is a celebration of what God has done and is doing in the life of this couple. _____ (groom) and _____ (bride) have asked me to express to you their deep love and gratitude for your support, your love, your concern, and your prayers. They have been blessed by God's gift of you in their lives. They ask that you now share in the joy of the reestablishment of their marriage.

THE INVOCATION

Gracious Lord, who heals and restores the broken, we praise you for your great mercy. Thank you for your divine intervention in our lives. Thank you for your patience when we fail to be all we should be as your adopted children. We praise you with joy unspeakable for the many times you have offered your forgiveness for our shortcomings and our sin. We praise you, for you alone are worthy of our praise and adoration. We pray that your presence will be known and honored in these sacred moments. We pray these things with confidence, for we trust in the restorative power, work, and name of Jesus Christ. Amen.

THE CONGREGATIONAL HYMN

Great Is Thy Faithfulness

THE MEDITATION ON REMARRIAGE

You two have tasted the joy of marriage when it was sweet and satisfying. Your cup was full and overflowed with love for each other and the Lord. You have also tasted of marriage when it became bitter and sour. You have seen your cup dashed and broken as your love for each other and the Lord was spilled and about to dry up. Yet in his infinite love, God has reached down, picked up the broken vessel, and carefully examined it to see where the weaknesses lie and how it was broken.

While not presuming that we have the mind of God, we, as believers and as his children made in his image, are enabled to have the wisdom to understand important truths. We are told in 1 Corinthians: "The spiritual man makes judgments about all things. . . . we have the mind of Christ" (1 Cor. 2:15*a*–16*b*). Let us, therefore, be led by the Holy Spirit to how the vessel of marriage is broken:

The vessel is broken through neglect. If you've ever stepped inside a dilapidated and abandoned home, you can see the pervasive evidence of neglect. Among those objects of neglect often found in this setting are broken windows, broken boards, broken furniture, broken glasses, and broken dishes. I'm sure the former owner of such a home never planned on seeing his home and belongings in such disrepair or imagined seeing such broken remains of his dreams. I know of no one who marries with the intention of neglecting the marriage. Yet, when we look around our world, we see the pervasive evidence of neglect. We see the broken promises, the broken vows, the broken hearts, the broken lives, and the broken dreams.

What happened to such a vessel of marriage? One or both partners neglected to do all they had pledged to do to make the marriage the beautiful and solid vessel it was intended to be. More often than not, one or both partners neglected their relationship to—and reliance upon—God, who is the glue that holds marriages—and lives—together.

The vessel is broken through stress. You have heard it said so many times: "Life is tough." _____ (groom) and _____ (bride), you know that to be true. You have known the stress factors that can cause a marriage to break, and you may have even known the stress factors that can cause an individual to break. The world delights in our assuming all the roles and handling all the pressures it can dole out to us. Often we are driven to do more, and then we want more. If we want more, then we do whatever it takes to acquire that which we desire. This may lead us no longer to desire God's best for our lives. We may desire that which should be—or is—forbidden for us. Then, we may choose to escape it all in ways that may or may not be God-honoring. And we—and our marriages—may eventually break under the stress.

The vessel is broken through abuse. This is a tragic way in which the vessel of marriage is broken or destroyed. One or both partners no longer treats the other with the care and respect deserved; instead, he or she sinfully and willfully abuses the other with words or deeds. Marriage should be treated with the same care and devotion as a cherished stem of the finest crystal. One would not think of shattering the crystal vessel with a hammer. Neither should a marriage take the hammering of abuse.

There is good news for the broken. God uses the words of the psalmist to speak to us: "I have become like broken pottery . . . but I trust in you, O LORD; I say, 'You are my God.' My times are in your hands" (Ps. 31:12*b*, 14–15*a*). The prophet Isaiah instructed the broken to call upon the Lord and seek his forgiving restoration: "O LORD, you are our Father. We are the clay, you are the potter; we are all the work of your hand. Do not be angry beyond measure, O LORD; do not remember our sins forever. Oh, look upon us, we pray" (Isa. 64:8–9*a*). How does God receive us in our brokenness? Again, the psalmist ministers to us when he writes: "The sacrifices of God are a broken spirit; a broken and contrite heart, O God, you will not despise" (Ps. 51:17). Good news! The God of grace and mercy gives second chances—and many more. Our coming to him with—and as—broken vessels is like our offering him the sweetest, most acceptable sacrifice.

How, then, does our loving Father, the Master Potter, restore the broken vessel of marriage?

The vessel is restored by grace. The broken vessel of marriage—or a life—can be restored by the Master Potter's gracious touch and shaping. He alone can take that vessel which is broken and restore it to its previous glory—or to even greater beauty and usefulness. _____ (groom) and _____ (bride), you have sought the gracious work of God in your lives and in your relationship. You have acknowledged that you are not able to do this without his gracious work in your hearts and lives. Hear, then, and heed these comforting words from the book of Hebrews: "Let us then approach the throne of grace with confidence, so that we may receive mercy and find grace to help us in our time of need" (4:16).

The vessel is restored by forgiveness. _____ (groom) and _____ (bride), you have sought the forgiveness of God and each other as you have sought to restore the broken vessel of your marriage. This necessary step is more than just saying, "I'm sorry." Your seeking forgiveness must be accompanied by true repentance: a true turning from erroneous ways, from sinful choices in lifestyle or action, and from putting your desires and feelings above that of your mate's or above God's will.

The vessel is restored by commitment. _____ (groom) and _____ (bride), you stand before us, ready to recommit yourselves to restoring your marriage and preserving your love. As you are well aware, for a marriage to stay whole and functioning, it demands great care. Earlier we mentioned the necessity of attention always being given to your partner and your marriage. Unconditional love, unending devotion, and untainted faithfulness must also be consistently demonstrated to your partner, if your marriage vessel is to be restored and to remain unbroken.

You cannot afford to overlook your individual relationships to God, for marriage partners cannot neglect their private devotion and prayer, their consistent study of—and obedience to—God's Word, and their corporate expression of worship if they are to grow in their relationship with the Master Potter. The attitude of the psalmist must be the attitude of one committed to a solid vessel of marriage: "I rejoice in following your statutes as one rejoices in great riches. I meditate on your precepts and consider your ways. I delight in your decrees; I will not neglect your word" (Ps. 119:14–16). Let your love for—and commitment to—each other grow out of your love for—and commitment to—God.

THE EXCHANGE OF VOWS

_____ (groom), is it your desire to see the broken vessel of your marriage to _____ (bride) restored by the power of the Master Potter, our Lord and Savior?

Groom responds: "It is."

Then, _____ (groom), repeat after me these vows of restoration and recommitment:

Groom: "I, _____ (groom), stand before God and these witnesses to reaffirm my love for you and to recommit my life to being a godly husband. I promise to honor you, cherish you, and serve you all the days of my life. I pledge that I will never leave or forsake you. By

God's power and grace, I will seek to build with you a home of lasting joy, peace, and security. With thanksgiving in my heart, I take you, _____ (bride), to be my wedded wife from this day forth."

_____ (bride), is it your desire to see the broken vessel of your marriage to _____ (groom) restored by the power of the Master Potter, our Lord and Savior?

Bride responds: "It is."

Then, _____ (bride), repeat after me these vows of restoration and recommitment:

Bride: "I, _____ (bride), stand before God and these witnesses to reaffirm my love for you and to recommit my life to being a godly wife. I promise to honor you, cherish you, and serve you all the days of my life. I pledge that I will never leave or forsake you. By God's power and grace, I will seek to build with you a home of lasting joy, peace, and security. With thanksgiving in my heart, I take you, _____ (groom), to be my wedded husband from this day forth."

THE EXCHANGE OF RINGS

You have previously given and received rings, but these rings lost their original meaning for you. You have chosen not to wear your former rings; instead, you have chosen to give and receive new rings, bright and shining—like the hope and confidence you have in your restored relationship and marriage. Let these rings always be a symbol of your recommitment to God and to each other.

_____ (groom), place this ring on _____'s (bride's) finger and repeat after me:

Groom: "I, _____ (groom), give you, _____ (bride), this ring as a symbol of the recommitment of my will, my heart, and my being to keeping the vows of remarriage made to you, my wife, and to Christ, my Lord."

_____ (bride), do you receive this ring as a token of your husband's restored love?

Bride responds: "I do."

_____ (bride), place this ring on _____'s (groom's) finger and repeat after me:

Bride: "I, _____ (bride), give you, _____ (groom), this ring as a symbol of the recommitment of my will, my heart, and my being to keeping the vows of remarriage made to you, my husband, and to Christ, my Lord."

_____ (groom), do you receive this ring as a token of your wife's restored love?

Groom responds: "I do."

THE SONG AND PRAYER OF CONSECRATION

(The couple will kneel as the song is sung and remain kneeling throughout the song and the prayer of consecration.)

Have Thine Own Way, Lord (stanzas 1, 2, 4)

Have thine own way, Lord, in the lives and marriage of _____ (groom) and _____ (bride). Graciously hold them in your care, as you masterfully mold them to conform to the image of Jesus Christ. Fill them with your Spirit and guide them as they recommit their lives to each other and to you. For it is in your powerful, restorative name that we pray. Amen.

THE PRONOUNCEMENT

_____ (groom) and _____ (bride), how glorious it has been to have witnessed your vows of recommitment to each other and your exchanging of rings symbolizing your remarriage to each other! How magnificent is has been to see God's gracious restorative work in both of your lives! It is now a distinct privilege to pronounce that you are husband and wife forevermore. _____ (groom), you may kiss your wife.

THE BENEDICTION

Go forth now in the power of the Son, the peace of the Holy Spirit, and confidence in the Father's completing the good work begun in you and your marriage. Amen.

THE RECESSIONAL

THE POSTLUDE

Heaven in Our Home

A Ceremony for a Double Wedding
(This ceremony may be modified for a single wedding.)

———— ❧ ————

THE PRELUDE

THE PROCESSIONAL

(Bride 1, her father, and her attendants first process. Then the pastor will ask everyone to be seated. Next, bride 2, her father, and her attendants will process.)

THE CHIMING OF THE HOUR

THE SOLO AND THE LIGHTING OF THE CANDLES

(The mothers are escorted down the aisle to the front of the church, where they light the candles. They are then escorted to their seats.)

THE WELCOME

Beloved friends in Christ, this special moment has finally arrived. It is one about which these couples have dreamed, shared their thoughts with each other, and planned. Much love and joy has been theirs as they have anticipated this day. This once-in-a-lifetime experience is to be mutually shared by these two couples: as _____ (brothers or sisters), as a new extended family, and as friends who love each other enough to join together before God in these sacred moments. We stand before our heavenly Father to ask him to bless us with his affirming presence, to confirm his plan for these lives, and to add his divine favor to their unions.

THE STATEMENT OF AFFIRMATION

Let me begin by asking you a question: "Do you acknowledge the lordship of Christ in your life? And do you believe it to be God's will for you to marry?"

Both couples answer aloud together: "I do," or "We do."

Dear friends, it is almighty God that _____ (groom 1) and _____ (bride 1), _____ (groom 2) and _____ (bride 2) love with all their hearts. It is in the presence of this one true God that we have met today.

THE INVOCATION

Let us join our hearts in prayer: Good and holy God, we come into your presence with thanksgiving and praise. We bless you for the assurance of your guidance in our lives. We praise you for the awareness that you care about every endeavor of our lives, especially our relationships that lead to Christian marriage. Bless, then, this special occasion as _____ (groom 1) and _____ (bride 1), _____ (groom 2) and _____ (bride 2) come before you, their families, and friends to link their lives together in this ceremony of commitment. In Jesus' Name we pray. Amen.

THE CHARGE AND THE GIVING OF THE BRIDES

Marriage is built upon love, its virtue best portrayed in the thirteenth chapter of Paul's First Letter to the Corinthians: "Love is patient and kind; love is not jealous or boastful; it is not arrogant or rude. Love does not insist on its own way; it is not irritable or resentful; it does not rejoice at wrong, but rejoices in the right. Love bears all things, believes all things, hopes all things, endures all things. Love never ends. . . . So faith, hope, love abide, these three, but the greatest of these is love" (1 Cor. 13:4–8*a*, 13 RSV).

This sets a high standard for your relationship to each other. Your marriage must involve mutual concern and support, commitment and responsibility. Your love should emulate the love of Christ and his devotion to serve those whom he loved.

You are exhorted to dedicate your homes to your Lord and Savior, Jesus Christ. Take his Word, the Bible, for your guide. Also, give loyal devotion to his church. In faithfully doing these things, you will unite the great strengths of these two most important institutions, the home and his church. Live your lives as his willing servants, and true happiness will be your temporal and eternal reward.

_____ (groom 1), will you take _____ (bride 1) to be your wife? Will you commit yourself to her happiness and her self-fulfillment as a person and to her usefulness in God's kingdom work? Will you promise to love, honor, trust, and serve her in sickness and in health, in adversity and prosperity, and to be true and loyal to her, so long as you both shall live?

Groom 1 responds: "I do."

_____ (bride 1), will you take _____ (groom 1) to be your husband? Will you commit yourself to his happiness and his self-fulfillment as a person, and to his usefulness in God's kingdom work? Will you promise to love, honor, trust, and serve him in sickness and in health, in adversity and prosperity, and to be true and loyal to him, so long as you both shall live?

Bride 1 responds: "I do."

Believing you, _____ (groom 1) and _____ (bride 1), are committed to God's lordship in your lives and in your marriage, it is my privilege to ask, "Who gives this woman to be married to this man?"

Bride 1's father responds: "Her mother and I do."

(Groom 1 and bride 1 ascend to the upper platform, as father 1 is seated.)

_____ (groom 2), will you take _____ (bride 2) to be your wife? Will you commit yourself to her happiness and her self-fulfillment as a person and to her usefulness in God's kingdom work? Will you promise to love, honor, trust, and serve her in sickness and in health, in adversity and prosperity, and to be true and loyal to her, so long as you both shall live?

Groom 2 responds: "I do."

_____ (bride 2), will you take _____ (groom 2) to be your husband? Will you commit yourself to his happiness and his self-fulfillment as a person, and to his usefulness in God's kingdom work? Will you promise to love, honor, trust, and serve him in sickness and in health, in adversity and prosperity, and to be true and loyal to him, so long as you both shall live?

Bride 2 responds: "I do."

Believing you, _____ (groom 2) and _____ (bride 2), are committed to God's lordship in your lives and in your marriage, it is my privilege to ask, "Who gives this woman to be married to this man?"

Bride 2's father responds: "Her mother and I do."

(Groom 2 and bride 2 ascend to the upper platform, as father 2 is seated.)

THE STATEMENT OF MARRIAGE

Since God himself sanctified marriage when he brought together the first man and the first woman, since the Word of God speaks often of the honor and correctness of marriage, and because God promises blessings on those who are faithful to him and to each other, this then is a high and holy time for these children of God and for all who love them and share their hopes, prayers, and aspirations for a Christ-centered home and marriage.

All who come to the marriage altar desire to have a happy marriage. The nearest place to heaven in this world is a God-centered home. The opposite is also true. The nearest place to hell on earth is a house where hatred, bitterness, and strife are prominent. More scars are put upon a person's character and heart in an unhappy home than in any other place. There's no place like home! Someone said that a home ruled by God's Word is a place where visiting angels would not find themselves out of place. I know that is the kind of home you all desire. You want heaven in your homes. Three ingredients are needed in every marriage in order to put heaven in your homes.

The first ingredient is a present, a gift. Presents are always important to commemorate special occasions, as well as those days that are not "special," except that they are opportunities to express your love to your mate in a tangible way. Do not neglect the giving of presents to each other. Even more important than these material expressions of your love are those gifts that are nonmaterial: the giving of yourself, of your time, the giving of your devotion, of your total commitment. These are powerful ways to tell your mate: "I love you above all others." Important, too, are the gifts of praying for each other, of unselfish behavior and service toward your mate, and of desiring that your mate becomes all he or she is capable of becoming in Christ. Our Lord taught us this lifestyle of giving with his instructions: "It is more blessed to give than to receive" (Acts 20:35).

The second ingredient is purpose. Everyone needs a purpose. Every couple needs a purpose in order to put heaven in their home. A successful, godly marriage is not two people standing eye to eye—rather, shoulder to shoulder, looking toward similar goals. Competition is good in many areas, but it can kill a marriage. By meaningfully worshiping together, persistently praying, and honestly communicating, you can discover God's purpose for your lives and your home. I enjoin you to obey Jesus, who commands his followers, "Seek ye first the kingdom of God . . . and all these things shall be added unto you" (Matt. 6:33 KJV).

The third ingredient is power. The power behind a successful marriage is a person, Jesus Christ. He is the One who can put heaven in your home. In some cultures, the word *home* means "a shrine of the gods." In the Christian vocabulary, *home* means "the sanctuary or haven where Jesus Christ is Lord." A home cannot be successful if money, prestige, activities, or even loved ones are more important than Jesus. Without Christ as the focus of your lives and your home, your marriage will probably fail. With Christ as the power in your lives and home, your marriage cannot fail.

Jesus promised: "I am with you always, to the very end of the age" (Matt 28:20, NASB).

Heaven in the home . . . you can have heaven in your home with these three ingredients: the presents, the purpose, and the power.

THE VOWS

Believing you desire heaven in your home and trusting in your commitment to keep the vows you make today, I ask, "Are you ready to receive one another as a gift from God and to exchange your wedding vows?"

Both couples respond: "We are."

_____ (groom 1), repeat after me:

Groom 1: "I, _____ (groom 1), take you, _____ (bride 1), to be my cherished wife, to walk beside you when things are good and when things are bad. I accept you as a precious gift from God. Through God's power and with a desire to fulfill his purposes in our marriage, I will seek to demonstrate the love of Christ to you. All I have or hope to have I give to you as my life partner. I pledge you my unrivaled support, my persistent prayers, my unconditional love, and my constant faithfulness for as long as I live."

_____ (bride 1), repeat after me:

Bride 1: "I, _____ (bride 1), take you, _____ (groom 1), to be my cherished husband, to walk beside you when things are good and when things are bad. I accept you as a precious gift from God. Through God's power and with a desire to fulfill his purposes in our marriage, I will seek to demonstrate the love of Christ to you. All I have or hope to have, I give to you as my life partner. I pledge you my unrivaled support, my persistent prayers, my unconditional love, and my constant faithfulness for as long as I live."

_____ (groom 2), repeat after me:

Groom 2: "I, _____ (groom 2), take you, _____ (bride 2), to be my cherished wife, to walk beside you when things are good and when things are bad. I accept you as a precious gift from God. Through God's power and with a desire to fulfill his purposes in our marriage, I will seek to demonstrate the love of Christ to you. All I have or hope to have, I give to you as my life partner. I pledge you my unrivaled support, my persistent prayers, my unconditional love, and my constant faithfulness for as long as I live."

_____ (bride 2), repeat after me:

Bride 2: "I, _____ (bride 2), take you, _____ (groom 2), to be my cherished husband, to walk beside you when things are good and when things are bad. I accept you as a precious gift from God. Through God's power and with a desire to fulfill his purposes in our marriage, I will seek to demonstrate the love of Christ to you. All I have or hope to have, I give to you as my life partner. I pledge you my unrivaled support, my persistent prayers, my unconditional love, and my constant faithfulness for as long as I live."

THE RINGS

You have shared beautiful and powerful vows. You will now give and exchange rings as symbols of these vows of faith and love. A marriage ring says, "I love one person more dearly than all others. I am committed as a life partner to this person." A marriage ring is an outward symbol of an inner commitment, just as baptism symbolizes conversion. Let your marriage ring, therefore, from this time forward, remind you of the gift of God you have in your mate, the purpose of realizing heaven in your home, and the power of Christ you have in your marriage.

Now, _____ (groom 1), will you give _____ (bride 1) her ring and repeat after me this vow?

Groom 1: "With this ring I thee wed, and with it I give thee my faithfulness and devotion. I promise I will love you forever, for my love is of Christ. In the name of the Father, the Son, and the Holy Spirit."

Now, _____ (bride 1), will you give _____ (groom 1) his ring and repeat after me this vow?

Bride 1: "With this ring I thee wed, and with it I give thee my faithfulness and devotion. I promise I will love you forever, for my love is of Christ. In the name of the Father, the Son, and the Holy Spirit."

Now, _____ (groom 2), will you give _____ (bride 2) her ring and repeat after me this vow?

Groom 2: "With this ring I thee wed, and with it I give thee my faithfulness and devotion. I promise I will love you forever, for my love is of Christ. In the name of the Father, the Son, and the Holy Spirit."

Now, _____ (bride 2), will you give _____ (groom 2) his ring and repeat after me this vow?

Bride 2: "With this ring I thee wed, and with it I give thee my faithfulness and devotion. I promise I will love you forever, for my love is of Christ. In the name of the Father, the Son, and the Holy Spirit."

THE SONG AND PRAYER OF COMMITMENT

Let us pray.

(Both couples will kneel on their kneeling benches for this time of prayer. A song will be sung during these moments of silent prayer. Following the song, the minister will conclude the time of prayer by praying aloud.)

Dear Father, we come to you through Jesus Christ, the supreme manifestation of your love. We praise and thank you for the lives of _____ (groom 1) and _____ (bride 1), _____ (groom 2) and _____ (bride 2). We rejoice in their salvation and in their commitment to you. We bless you for their public declaration of faith, love, and devotion to you and to each other. We are grateful for their families and their friends who have expressed their love to them in countless ways over the years.

We ask that the three ingredients of a heaven-filled home never elude their grasp: presenting themselves, their time, and their devotion as gifts to their mate; the dedication to your purpose for their marriage; and the utilization of your power for their lives. May their homes so exemplify Christ that others will be strengthened and encouraged by the godly light shining through their lives and from their homes. For we pray and ask these things in the name that is above every name: Jesus Christ, our Lord. Amen.

(Both couples stand at the conclusion of the prayer and walk over to the two sets of unity candles.)

THE UNITY CANDLE

The two outside candles, representing your lives to this moment, have been selected and lit by your mothers. They are two distinct lights, each capable of going their own separate ways. To bring joy and harmony to your home, there must be the merging of these two lights into one. This is what the Lord meant when he said, "For this reason a man shall leave his father and mother and be joined to his wife, and the two shall become one" (Matt 19:5, RSV). From this point on, your thoughts shall be for each other rather than your individual selves. Your plans shall be mutual; your joys and sorrows shared alike.

_____ (groom 1) and _____ (bride 1), _____ (groom 2) and _____ (bride 2), take your individual candles from their holders and light the center candle as an expression of the purpose of your union: To grow in Christ and to radiate his love to all whose lives you touch. Do not extinguish your candles, but instead place them back in their original holders, still lit, symbolizing that your individual personalities remain, yet are merged as one with your mate.

THE SONG OF UNITY

(A song will be played or sung as both couples light their unity candles.)

THE PRONOUNCEMENT

_____ (groom 1) and _____ (bride 1), _____ (groom 2) and _____ (bride 2), God's Word teaches, "We love because he first loved us" (1 John 4:19). Because you have received Christ Jesus as your Lord and Savior, because you are committed to building a heaven-filled home, because you have pledged your faith in—and love to—each other, because you have sealed these marital vows by giving and receiving rings, acting in the authority vested in me by the laws of this state and looking to heaven for divine sanction, I now pronounce you husband and wife in the presence of God and these assembled witnesses. May the peace of God rule in your hearts and in your homes. _____ (groom 1) and _____ (groom 2), you may kiss your brides.

THE PRESENTATION

It is my pleasure to introduce and to present to you, Mr. and Mrs. _____ (groom 1's full name), and Mr. and Mrs. _____ (groom 2's full name).

THE RECESSIONAL

THE POSTLUDE

My Lifetime Love

A Ceremony for the Renewal of Wedding Vows
A Ceremony for Wedding Anniversaries

———— ✾ ————

THE PROCESSIONAL

THE WELCOME

We welcome you to this service of the renewal of the vows of marriage that _____ (husband) and _____ (wife) made _____ (number) years ago. This wonderful couple desires to reaffirm publicly their sacred promises before God, family, and friends. They are grateful to God who is the God of renewal. The psalmist reminds us of that wonderful reality when he writes: "Create in me a pure heart, O God, and renew a steadfast spirit within me" (Ps. 51:10).

THE PRAYER

Our God, Creator and Sustainer of all life, we are grateful that you make all things new. We recognize that you alone give rebirth to our spirits to fashion us for eternal life, that some day you will renew the heavens and the earth, that you transform and renew our minds, and that you renew our strength to enable us to make fresh steps of faith and commitment. We praise you for refreshing renewal! We pray that you will bless this unique time of renewal as _____ (husband) and _____ (wife) joyfully remember the past, optimistically look to the future, and humbly experience your presence now in this ceremony of renewal. In Jesus' name. Amen.

TIME OF REMEMBRANCE

Let's take a walk down memory lane. I want you to hold hands and remember:

- the first time you held hands,
  - your first kiss,
    - your wedding day,
      - your first home,
        - your first crisis,
          - your first child,
            - your first memorable vacation, and
              - your first shared grief.

Would you now face each other, with both hands joined, and together, before these witnesses, thank God for the life you have shared? *(The minister will prompt the couple.)*

Couple in unison repeats: "We thank you, God, for

the hopes and dreams,

stillness and sounds,

burdens and blessings,

pleasure and pain,

heartaches and hope,

> mountains and valleys,
>
> gladness and sorrow,
>
> grace and goodness,
>
> love and faith. Amen."

THE RENEWAL OF VOWS

As you continue to hold hands, _____ (husband), please repeat these vows of renewal and commitment to _____ (wife) after me:

Husband: "_____, (bride), thank you for being my devoted wife, my dearest friend, my desirable mate, and my dynamic partner. I am grateful for the faithful devotion you have shown as well as the unselfish sacrifices you have made for me (*if applicable:* "and our family"). I thank God for you and his blessing of my marriage to you for the past _____ (number) years. I consider it a privilege to stand with—and by—you. I joyfully recommit my love and my faithful devotion to you. I pledge to strive to grow in my faith and in my love of God, as I encourage you in your walk with the Lord. I promise I will not compromise my wedding vows. I will continue to love, honor, and cherish you as long as we both shall live. I pledge to join with you in creating a climate in our home that blesses family and friends. I promise to serve you, as together we serve God by serving others. Before these witnesses and in the presence of God, I now renew my wedding vows and declare that you alone are my lifetime love."

_____ (wife), please repeat these vows of renewal and commitment to _____ (husband) after me:

Wife: "_____, (groom), thank you for being my devoted husband, my dearest friend, my desirable mate, and my dynamic partner. I am grateful for the faithful devotion you have shown as well as the unselfish sacrifices you have constantly made for me (*if applicable, add:* "and our family"). I thank God for you and his blessing of my marriage to you for the past _____ (number) years. I consider it a privilege to stand with—and by—you. I joyfully recommit my love and my faithful devotion to you. I pledge to strive to grow in my faith and in my love of God, as I encourage you in your walk with the Lord. I promise I will not compromise my wedding vows. I will continue to love, honor, and cherish you as long as we both shall live. I pledge to join with you in creating a climate in our home that blesses family and friends. I promise to serve you, as together we serve God by serving others. Before these witnesses and in the presence of God, I now renew my wedding vows and declare that you alone are my lifetime love."

THE RENEWAL OF THE RINGS

Would you both now turn and face me? You are about to place again these rings, which have become increasingly meaningful symbols to you with the passing of years, upon your marriage partner's finger as you did _____ (number) years ago. A poet, more eloquent than I, beautifully expresses some tender thoughts about the hand that he held:

"This is the hand on which I placed
    A golden wedding ring,
The hand in which I placed my life,
    My love, my everything.

This is the hand that gave me strength
    To help me through the years,
The hand that touched me tenderly
    And wiped away the tears.

This is the hand that held our child
    So gently to her breast,
The hand that soothes away the pain
    And tenderly caressed.

This is the hand that pointed out
    The way our child should go,

The hand that gently led the way
   To make the loving grow.

This is the hand, the only hand,
   That I will ever hold,
The hand that I will hold in mine
   As all the years unfold.

This is the hand that wears my ring
   In happiness and pride,
Just as she did that day
   When she became my bride."[1]

_____ (wife), place your husband's wedding band on his finger. _____ (husband), repeat after me: "As I once again receive
this ring which you gave me as a symbol of our wedding vows
_____ (number) years ago, I promise that I will always gratefully
and proudly wear it. I assure you that all I possess and all I am continue
to belong to you. In the name of the Father, the Son, and the Holy
Spirit. Amen."

_____ (husband), place your wife's wedding band on her
finger. _____ (wife), repeat after me: "As I once again receive
this ring which you gave me as a symbol of our wedding vows
_____ (number) years ago, I promise that I will always gratefully and proudly wear it. I assure you that all I possess and all I am
continue to belong to you. In the name of the Father, the Son, and the
Holy Spirit. Amen."

THE PRAYER OF RENEWAL

Dear Lord of renewal, would you continue to bless the home of
_____ (husband) and _____ (wife)? May their children
[and children's children (*if applicable*)] be a blessing to them and a forever heritage of the Lord. We praise you that the gates of hell cannot
prevail against such a committed love built on Jesus Christ, the solid
rock, the foundation of this home. You have heard these vows. May

every promise be secured by God in heaven and earth. In Jesus' eternal name we pray. Amen.

THE PRONOUNCEMENT

Forasmuch as _____ (husband) and _____ (wife) together have consented to continue in the bonds of faith and love; have witnessed the same before God, their beloved family, and cherished friends; have given and exchanged their vows and rings as public symbols of their renewed promises; it is my joy to announce that they continue to be husband and wife, now and until the day they meet Jesus Christ. Amen!

_____ (husband) kiss _____ (wife), your sweetheart, best friend, bride, and wife forever.

THE RECESSIONAL

Renewing Our Marriage Covenant

A Ceremony for Congregational Covenant/Vow Renewal
(This ceremony can be easily adapted as a covenant/vow renewal ceremony for individual couples.)

THE PRELUDE

THE WELCOME

Church family, friends, those who come to renew their marriage covenants (*or* vows), and their loved ones, we welcome you to this special covenant (*or* vow) renewal service. This is a time of celebration of what God has done in and through the unions of these couples who are here to recommit themselves to their mates and to God. This is a time of introspection for each of us who are married as we each examine our own lives to see if we are fulfilling the covenants (*or* vows) that we have made with our mate and with God. This is a solemn time of worship and of covenant (*or* vow) renewal in the presence of our holy and supreme God to be witnessed by each of you.

THE PROCESSIONAL (OPTIONAL)

(Participating couples will process to the front of the church.)

THE INVOCATION

(If there is no processional of couples, ask couples to come to the front of the church or to stand at their seats.)

Let us pray: God of Heaven and Earth, we bow before you in recognition that you alone are sovereign and that you alone rule and reign over this universe. We thank you, Lord, that you orchestrate the events of life, all of which you use to accomplish your good and pleasing purpose. We put our trust in your supremacy as together we come to witness the covenant (*or* vow) renewals that these couples are about to make in your good name. We ask that you would bless this time, that all we are about to do would bring honor to you, and that this sacred ceremony would reaffirm the love and commitment of these marriage partners. Gracious God, draw us now into your holy presence. For it is in Jesus' name we pray. Amen.

THE WEDDING CHARGE

This ceremony of marriage covenant (*or* vow) renewal is not to be lightly regarded, but rather prayerfully and reverently approached. It is a holy service in which three solemn tasks will be accomplished:

We will recognize the character of the God we serve as we worship him in this sacred ceremony of covenant (or vow) renewal. In the sixth chapter of Isaiah, the words of the prophet are recorded: "I saw the Lord seated on a throne, high and exalted, and the train of his robe filled the temple" (Isa. 6:1). Isaiah had an extraordinary vision of God majestically sitting on his throne, the highest, most exalted throne in all the universe. Today, we, too, recognize that our God is sovereign above all, and for that reason we submit to his absolute authority. As subjects of our sovereign Lord, we are urged by the apostle Paul to submit to God's divine authority and plan for our lives: "Therefore, I urge you, brothers, in view of God's mercy, to offer your bodies as living sacrifices, holy and pleasing to God—this is your spiritual act of worship. Do not conform any longer to the pattern of this world, but be transformed by the renewing of your mind. Then you will be able to test and approve what God's will is—his good, pleasing and perfect will" (Rom. 12:1–2).

Submitting to his lordship, we, as Christians, should realize and acknowledge that there should be no distinction between the motives for our conduct in our secular life and in our religious life. We are always under God's authority. We are to serve and recognize him in every aspect of our lives. This is especially true in faithfully honoring the sacred marriage covenant (*or* vow) we have made. We are told in the Old Testament that those who keep their covenants with the sovereign God are blessed; those who do not keep their covenants will be punished. Our God is a God who delights in showing his favor for those who faithfully follow him and keep their covenants (*or* vows) made with him. Scripture tells us that every good and perfect gift comes from our Father above (James 1:17).

Therefore, we are to recognize God's faithfulness in blessing us and seek to understand his intentions for marriage. We know that a "good and perfect gift" for a husband is a faithful and godly wife who reflects the character of her Lord and Savior. Likewise, a "good and perfect gift" for a wife is a faithful and godly husband who reflects the character of his Lord and Savior. Couples, thank God that, as transformed children of the heavenly Father, you can embrace his promises, graciously receive his many blessings in your lives, and seek to know his good and perfect gift, his covenantal blessing in faithful Christian marriage.

We will rejoice with these couples in the celebration of marriage. In this age of "living together" and all-too-common divorce, marriage is something to be celebrated and elevated by the church. Marriage is the prime human bond, the foundation of all social order. The biblical teachings and examples of marriage describe marriage as: a divine institution, a companionship alliance, a romantic relationship, a sexual union, a joint livelihood, a common primary responsibility for parenting, a shared religious life, and a covenantal bond.[1]

Common to all these descriptions of marriage is the basic principle that in marriage two become one. We read in the Gospel of Mark: "For this reason a man will leave his father and mother and . . . become one flesh. So they are no longer two, but one" (Mark 10:7–8a). The biblical symbol of marital oneness suggests unity, a union—a fusion—of individual lives in a lasting bond. Couples, we celebrate your commitment to the one to whom you are united in marriage. We celebrate your enduring and growing love for each other and the Lord. We celebrate what God is doing in and through your lives, your families, and your Christian homes.

We will reaffirm and renew the most important of all human covenants, the marriage covenant. For God's children, the marriage relationship is a covenant between a man and a woman, not a contract. Malachi pictures God as "the witness between you and the wife of your youth . . . your partner, the wife of your marriage covenant" (Mal. 2:14). God initiated covenants with man at creation and established covenants throughout redemptive history. The permanence and faithfulness of God's promises are characteristic of his covenantal relationship with man. God's example of covenantal faithfulness and permanence provides the basis of the marriage covenant. This is the ideal for Christian marriage. We read in Song of Solomon a plea for permanence in the love relationship: "Place me like a seal over your heart, like a seal on your arm; for love is as strong as death, its jealousy unyielding as the grave. It burns like blazing fire, like a mighty flame. Many waters cannot quench love; rivers cannot wash it away. If one were to give all the wealth of his house for love, it would be utterly scorned" (Song of Sol. 8:6–8).

This image of a permanent bond is stated by Jesus as a command: "What therefore God hath joined together, let not man put asunder" (Mark 10:9 KJV). We find the biblical ideal for faithfulness in marriage is strongly stated in the Book of Malachi: "Has not the LORD made them one? In flesh and spirit they are his. And why one? Because he was seeking godly offspring. So guard yourself in your spirit, and do not break faith with the wife of your youth. 'I hate divorce,' says the LORD God of Israel" (2:15–16a). Couples, I charge you to recommit yourselves in these sacred moments to faithfully and permanently honoring the covenant between you and your mate, and witnessed by God.

THE VOWS

Couples, the seriousness of the vows you are about to renew must never be minimized; therefore, as you repeat after me, think soberly about the vows you are renewing. Husbands, face your wives and repeat after me:

Husbands: "Beloved wife, I thank God for our marriage. Today, in the presence of God and these witnesses, I renew my marriage covenant with you. I joyfully recommit myself to placing our relationship above all earthly relationships, to loving and cherishing you above all others, to serving and honoring you in a Christlike manner, to growing with you in our relationship with the Lord, and to faithfully staying with you as together we face all of life's circumstances for as long as we both shall live."

Wives, face your husbands and repeat after me:

Wives: "Beloved husband, I thank God for our marriage. Today, in the presence of God and these witnesses, I renew my marriage covenant with you. I joyfully recommit myself to placing our relationship above all earthly relationships, to loving and cherishing you above all others, to serving and honoring you in a Christlike manner, to growing with you in our relationship with the Lord, and to faithfully staying with you as together we face all of life's circumstances for as long as we both shall live."

THE EXCHANGE OF RINGS

Your wedding ring is an outward and visible sign of the marriage covenant you made with your mate. The ring has been used for centuries, by kings and rulers, to seal important covenants. As the most lasting symbol of marriage, your ring is a constant reminder of your commitment to this one who stands next to you. The refined precious metal in your ring represents the purity of faithful, untarnished covenant keeping. Your ring's unending, circular design represents the permanence of covenantal commitment. As you once again place your mate's ring on his or her hand, remember the blessings of God as your covenantal promises have been honored and pledge anew to keep the solemn covenant you made—and now renew—to the honor of God.

Husbands, do you give this ring anew to your wife as a symbol of the covenant you made with her and today renew?

Husbands respond: "I do."

Wives, do you receive this ring anew as a symbol of the covenant your husband made with you and today renews?

Wives respond: "I do."

Husbands, place your wife's wedding ring on her finger and repeat after me:

Husbands: "With this ring, I thee wed and sealed my vows in the honorable estate of marriage. I give it to you anew as a symbol of my covenant renewal with you and before God, and as a symbol of my unending love for you."

Wives, do you give this ring anew to your husband as a symbol of the covenant you made with him and today renew?

Wives respond: "I do."

Husbands, do you receive this ring anew as a symbol of the covenant your wife made with you and today renews?

Husbands respond: "I do."

Wives, place your husband's wedding ring on his finger and repeat after me:

Wives: "With this ring, I thee wed and sealed my vows in the honorable estate of marriage. I give it to you anew as a symbol of my covenant renewal with you and before God, and as a symbol of my unending love for you."

THE PRAYER AND SONG OF CONSECRATION

Let us pray.

(Couples who are able to do so should kneel during this time of prayer.)

Find Us Faithful (or another suitable selection)

God Almighty, gracious Covenant Maker and faithful Covenant Keeper, we ask that your Holy Spirit enable these couples faithfully to keep their solemn covenantal vows. We ask that you guard and protect these marriages for the lifetimes of these mates. We also ask that you remind each of us who have witnessed this ceremony that we, as the body of Christ, have a responsibility to be guardians of these unions. Give us the courage to challenge any of these who might forsake their vows or any from outside who might threaten these marriages. For it is in the strong and binding name of Jesus Christ, who gave his very life to fulfill God's covenantal promises to us, that we pray. Amen.

(Couples should stand and face the minister.)

THE PRONOUNCEMENT

Couples, because you have expressed your maturing love and devotion for each other; because you have promised before God and these witnesses faithfully to keep the solemn vows of your marriage covenant; because you have pledged to continue to honor, cherish, and serve each other all the days of your lives, it is my joy to affirm the renewal of your marriage covenant and to pronounce that you continue to be husband and wife. What God has joined together, let no one put asunder. Husbands, you may kiss your wives.

THE HYMN

Couples, please turn and face the congregation, as we all join in singing:

The Bond of Love (or another suitable hymn or chorus)

THE BENEDICTION

Loving Father, we thank you for your heavenly example of gracious and faithful covenant keeping. Precious Savior, we thank you for your earthly example of the same, even to the point of death. Holy Spirit, we thank you for your promise never to leave us or forsake us. Enable these couples faithfully to follow your divine example of covenant keeping and unconditional love. Complete the good work you have begun in their lives and marriages. Bless these couples as they honor you above all others by faithfully obeying the covenantal terms you have set before them. Bless these couples as they honor their mates by faithfully keeping the covenantal terms of their marriage vows. May grace, love, and peace abide now and always with you. Amen.

THE SIGNING OF THE MARRIAGE COVENANT RENEWAL

Couples, please join your family and loved ones for the signing of your marriage covenant renewal.

THE POSTLUDE

Best Friends for Life

—— ✦ ——

THE PROCESSIONAL

THE WELCOME

One of the Bible's great verses proclaims, "I was glad when they said unto me, Let us go into the house of the LORD" (Ps. 122:1). We *are* glad to be in the house of the Lord this day to share in the gladness of _____ (groom) and _____ (bride), as these best friends join their lives in a dynamic, new relationship: husband and wife—best friends for life. On their behalf, welcome. Thank you for multiplying their joy by sharing as they make their wedding vows.

THE INVOCATION

Let us ask the Lord of this house of worship for his blessing on this couple and this occasion: Father of glory, giver of all gladness and perfect joy through Jesus Christ, we are deeply conscious of your interest in the lives of _____ (groom) and _____ (bride) and in their hearts' desire to honor you on this day of days. We ask your blessing. We seek your pleasure. We offer our thanksgiving to you for the incredible richness of the lifetime investment of parents, grandparents, family, and friends into the lives of _____ (groom) and _____ (bride). Now, as we share in the dividends of these deposits, may we all be enriched by this blessed event. In the name of our precious Savior and Best Friend, who laid down his life for us, Jesus Christ. Amen.

THE GIVING OF THE BRIDE

An old minister used to preface a marriage ceremony by saying, "My friends, marriage is a curse to the many, a blessing to the few, and a great uncertainty to all. Do you venture?"[1] Believing that this couple considers marriage to be a blessing; that they have prayed, prepared, and planned for it to be such; and that they are confident they have the blessing of God and family, it is my privilege to ask, "Who gives this woman to be married to this man?"

Father responds: "Her mother and I give _____ (bride) in marriage."

THE TEACHING ON MARRIAGE AND FRIENDSHIP

A favorite scriptural passage chosen by couples for their wedding ceremony is found in Ruth 1:16–17: "But Ruth replied, 'Don't urge me to leave you or to turn back from you. Where you go I will go, and where you stay I will stay. Your people will be my people and your God my God. Where you die I will die, and there I will be buried. May the LORD deal with me, be it ever so severely, if anything but death separates you and me.'" It is interesting to discover that these were not words exchanged between husband and wife but between mother-in-law and daughter-in-law. Actually, their relationship was more than that, as Ruth and Naomi were really best friends.

Many couples who ultimately become husband and wife started out as "just friends." Very often there is the pattern of their being just friends, then close friends, and eventually best friends. Their friendship

leads to marriage, with their becoming the most intimate of friends—
and best friends for life. For marriage partners who are believers in
Jesus Christ, there's another dimension to their friendship. With their
union in Christ, they also become friends forever.

Friendships have been described and depicted in many ways.
Perhaps you have seen the small figurine of two baby kittens snuggling
up to each other with the statement, "Friendship is a special kind of
love," printed on its base. Or perhaps you have seen the sentiment, "True
friendships are such hard work, it is easy to understand why we have so
few of them," expressed on other artwork. _____ (groom) and
_____ (bride), how would you describe your friendship with each
other? Perhaps this sentiment, as expressed in a Valentine card, captures
and expresses the initial feelings you had for each other:

"When we first met, I didn't realize
   that we could become friends . . .
   we have different tastes,
   we look at life in different ways . . .
   But the more I get to know you,
   the more I like you.
You're caring, honest, supportive,
   and fun to be with . . .
   In fact, you're everything
   I hope for in a friend.
I'm really glad we took the time
   to get past things
   that make us different,
   so that I could discover in you
   a special friend."[2]

_____ (groom) and _____ (bride), no doubt your
friendship has gone way beyond this early stage of friendship. It is
important as you enter this new relationship of marriage that both of
you are committed to working hard at helping your friendship with

each other develop and grow, for it can slip through your fingers. Your friendship in marriage should be characterized by commitment, genuineness, joy, unique sense of "we-ness," trustworthiness, acceptance, intimacy, encouragement, positive personal regard, transcendence, and permanence.[3] If you are diligent in maintaining your friendship with each other, then, with the passing years, you will be able to say with great satisfaction, "My mate is not only my helper, lover, and companion but also my best friend for life."

There is at least one other dimension of your friendship that we should consider. You have proclaimed in faith that you both have a Friend above all other friends. He is the One who said, "Greater love has no one than this, that he lay down his life for his friends" (John 15:13). He is also the One who did that for us. He is God's own Son: Jesus, precious Friend and Savior. For those of us who call him Friend, our friendship with him passed through many normal stages.

At first, he seemed like a stranger to us, unless from early childhood we were introduced to him. With time, we began to see our need for him in our lives, a need to embrace him as Savior and dearest Friend. With that realization and our profession of faith in him, a great transformation took place in our relationship to him. We went from foe to friend in our relationship to Christ. One Christian author says, "I think the essence of the matter might be stated by saying that Christianity is the acceptance of the gift of the friendship of Jesus."[4] And truly it is.

_____ (groom) and _____ (bride), as you grow in your love and friendship with each other, never forsake the most important friendship in your lives—your relationship to Jesus Christ. As you grow in love and devotion to him, you will be better equipped to love and cherish each other as best friends for life.

THE VOWS

Let us celebrate your growing friendship with Christ and each other by the giving of your vows. Would you face your best friend?

_____ (groom), please repeat after me this vow made to _____ (bride).

Groom: "I, _____ (groom), because of my eternal friendship with Jesus Christ, do promise you, _____ (bride), to be your husband and best friend for all the years God has planned for us. I commit to you to make it my priority to bring glory to him through my own life and through our lives together. I will be faithful to you and will reserve the most intimate place in my life for you. I vow this in Jesus' name."

_____ (bride), please repeat after me this vow made to _____ (groom).

Bride: "I, _____ (bride), because of my eternal friendship with Jesus Christ, do promise you, _____ (groom), to be your wife and best friend for all the years God has planned for us. I commit to you to make it my priority to bring glory to him through my own life and through our lives together. I will be faithful to you and will reserve the most intimate place in my life for you. I vow this in Jesus' name."

THE RINGS

Most people love the giving and wearing of rings. Rings carry endorsements and messages of all kinds. Perhaps, in your childhood, you have worn with pride a secret decoder ring, the marketing product found in a box of Cracker Jacks. Or perhaps you have worn a smiley face ring or a mood ring. Rings are also symbolic of many important life events. You probably were excited the first time you placed your high school ring on your finger. Then, when you allowed that girlfriend or boyfriend to wear it, it brought you great pride. Premier athletes wear rings to show the world that they are national champions. Rings also are symbolic of cherished relationships. Maybe at some time in your life, you received a friendship ring. Today, you are giving and receiving the most elite of all symbols of friendship and of any human relationship: the wedding ring. As you give and receive this symbol, may it always be a reminder of your love and devotion to each other and to God.

_____ (groom), do you give this ring to _____ (bride) as a witness of your commitment as husband and of a growing love and friendship?

Groom responds: "I do."

_____ (groom), place the ring on _____'s (bride's) finger as you repeat this vow after me: "This ring I joyfully give to you as a lifelong symbol of my commitment to you, my wife and my best friend. I do this in the name of our Savior and precious Friend, Jesus Christ."

_____ (bride), do you give this ring to _____ (groom) as a witness of your commitment as wife and of a growing love and friendship?

Wife responds: "I do."

_____ (bride), place the ring on _____'s (groom's) finger as you repeat this vow after me: "This ring I joyfully give to you as a lifelong symbol of my commitment to you, my wife and my best friend. I do this in the name of our Savior and precious Friend, Jesus Christ."

THE BENEDICTION

Oh God, what a Friend we have in Jesus! Thank you for the gift of your divine friendship! Thank you for teaching us what true love and friendship is all about. Now, dear Lord of our hearts, seal this service with your grace and power, and enable _____ (groom) and _____ (bride) to keep their promise to be devoted to their marriage relationship and to be best friends for life. Allow them to grow in ever-deepening friendship with each other and with you. For it is in Jesus' name that we ask these things. Amen.

THE PRONOUNCEMENT

Believing that it is the resolve of your hearts to be husband and wife and to grow a friendship that brings glory to God, joy to your family, and encouragement to others, I pronounce that from this time forward, you are husband and wife. Our prayers and love, encouragement and friendship go with you.

I am happy to present to you Mr. and Mrs. _____, best friends for life.

THE RECESSIONAL

A Love that Lasts

———— ✦ ————

THE PRELUDE

(Vocal and Organ/Instrumental Music)

THE CHIMING OF THE HOUR

THE SEATING OF THE GRANDPARENTS

(Song of praise is to be sung as the grandparents are seated.)

THE SEATING OF THE PARENTS

(Song of thanksgiving is to be sung as the parents are seated.)

THE ENTRANCE OF THE GROOMSMEN

(The minister, groom, and groomsmen enter as the processional begins.)

THE PROCESSIONAL

THE CALL TO CELEBRATION

Dear family and friends, we have gathered to celebrate one of life's most significant events: the joining of two lives into one, the celebration of marriage. _____ (groom) and _____ (bride) are grateful for your presence and your support on this important day in their lives. They believe that God has led them to each other as part of his wonderful plan for their lives. It is their desire to affirm their vows to each other and before God in your presence.

THE INVOCATION

Join me in prayer as we ask God's blessing on this exceptional moment in their lives. Let us pray: Author and Perfecter of life and love, thank you for this day of days in _____'s (groom's) and _____'s (bride's) life journey. We thank you for your presence that you promised for those gathered in your name. We thank you for this couple's parents who gave them life and love. We thank you for their friends who have encouraged them along the way. We thank you for your church that has taught and led them in the faith. We thank you for your will that introduced them to each other. We thank you for genuine love that only comes from you and lasts forever. We thank you for the sense of expectancy that excites us in this love. We ask your blessing and guidance as we unite _____ (groom) and _____ (bride) in marriage. In the name of eternal love, Jesus Christ, we pray. Amen.

THE WEDDING CHARGE

In the quiet Garden of Eden, God made man in his own image (Gen. 1:27). The Bible, however, tells us that God saw that it was not good for the man to be alone (Gen. 2:18). So, with loving care, he removed a bone from Adam's side from which to fashion Eve. And God brought Eve to Adam (Gen. 2:21–22) to be his wife.

Scripture suggests that God specifically made Eve for Adam and Adam for Eve. _____ (groom) and _____ (bride), you have both affirmed that you believe God specifically purposed you to share life together and that he, too, made you for each other. As an acknowledgment that you do receive one another as God's gift of life and love, please join hands.

_____ (groom), it is important for a husband to learn something about receiving his wife by observing the manner in which God created Eve. God did not use a bone from Adam's foot to suggest he should "lord it over" the wife, nor did he take a bone from his head to suggest that Eve should "lord it over" the husband. In choosing to use Adam's rib, it is suggested that Eve was created to share life at Adam's side, close to his heart. Also, since Adam was first created, it is suggested that God intended man to initiate spiritual leadership in the home.

_____ (groom), is it your commitment to receive _____ (bride) to your side, to love her and care for her, to open your heart and life to her, and to be the spiritual leader in the home? Do you so promise?

Groom responds: "I do."

_____ (bride), the wife learns something important about her role in marriage and how to receive her husband by also observing the order of creation. Inasmuch as God chose first to create man, then from man made a woman, and brought her to man, it is suggested that God intended woman truly to consider herself as a gift to man. According to New Testament teaching, a wife must trust her husband as the leader in the home. This means that a wife must be submissive to her husband's spiritual authority and leadership in the home.

_____ (bride) is it your commitment to receive _____ (groom) as your spiritual head and be submissive to his leadership as his supportive and loving wife? Do you so promise?

Bride responds: "I do."

THE GIVING OF THE BRIDE

Believing that the home you wish to establish is founded on these biblical principles of love, it is my privilege to ask who gives this woman to be married to this man?

Father responds: "Her mother and I do."

THE SONG OF COMMITMENT

(Bride and groom walk up steps from the floor to the platform level as the song begins.)

THE STATEMENT OF MARRIAGE

On days like today, it is important to ask, "What makes a marriage last?" The answer is as basic as building a house or any structure. Be sure it has a solid foundation. Foundational qualities that will stand the test of time are necessary for building a marriage and home that lasts. What are these foundational qualities of a love that lasts?

A love that lasts is a marriage built on true commitment of love. This kind of love is not built upon feelings or expectancies, but is possible only through "God-love." This kind of love, "God-love," rises above selfishness and feelings. It desires the highest welfare of the other person. Some of its dimensions are described in 1 Corinthians 13 (vv. 4–8, TMNT).

"Love never gives up." It is a love that is able to endure illnesses, problems, losses, job changes, relocations, and disappointments. It is a love that keeps on keeping on. "Love isn't always 'me first,' doesn't fly off the handle." It is a love that isn't resentful or irritable. It is a love that doesn't carry a chip on its shoulder. It is love that drains bitterness quickly. "Puts up with anything." It is a love that knows when and how to keep silent in the face of criticism or neglect and doesn't parade the weakness of your mate to others. "Always looks for the best." It is a love that believes in the goodness and purity of a mate's motives and intentions toward the other when temporary discouragements occur. "Keeps going to the end. Love never dies." It is a love that persists, is tenacious, and will endure, despite all odds. It is a love that does not let up. It is a love that understands the importance of "hanging in there" and not running away.

A love that lasts is a marriage built on faith in God alone. You begin today to build a household of faith. Every person is, at heart, intensively spiritual. It has been said there is a God-shaped vacuum in the heart of every person that cannot be satisfied by any created thing. It can only be filled by Creator God, who makes himself known to the person through the person of Jesus Christ. God's provision for your spiritual vacuum is Jesus Christ, who said, "I am the way, and the truth and the life. No one comes to the Father except through me" (John 14:6, TMNT).

Just as you were born physically, you both have recognized your need to be born spiritually. You both have found that new life in the regenerating—the being "born again"—work of Jesus Christ. You have both proclaimed that Jesus Christ is your Lord and Savior and earnestly seek to follow him. Your marriage will grow stronger and last longer as you both personally grow in your faith, devotion, and service to God.

A love that lasts is a marriage built on "heroic love." The term "heroic love" is what one author uses to refer to a love that sacrifices itself for the enrichment of the other person.[1] Jesus said it this way: "This is my command: Love one another the way I loved you. This is the very best way to love. Put your life on the line for your friends" (John 15:12–13, TMNT). An amazing reality about this kind of love is that it does not leave the giver empty, but it carries with it a power-fully revitalizing capacity. In the dark and bright days, in the cold and hot seasons, in the mountains and in the valleys, the love that never fades is built on a love that always gives. With this type of love in your marriage, you can say with Rudyard Kipling: "Love like ours can never die."[2]

THE VOWS

Are you now ready to face one another, join hands, and repeat your vows to the Lord and to each other?

Groom and bride respond: "We are."

Then face one another, join hands, and repeat after me:

Groom: I, _____ (groom), commit myself to you, _____ (bride), as your husband. As Jesus molds my love for you into the kind of love he has for his church, I promise to love you with a maturing Christlike love. I receive you as my cherished wife, acknowledging that you are a precious gift from the Father and that with you I am better able to glorify God than apart from you. Next to my relationship to God, my relationship to you is most dear to me. I promise to lead you as together we grow to love the Lord, our God, with all our heart, soul, mind, and strength. I promise to hold you, to listen to you, to care for you, and to encourage you. In our marriage, I promise to be transparently open with you and to communicate honestly with you. I will work with you in making our home a place of refuge, peace, and comfort. I will seek always to show gentleness and kindness, patience, and joy toward you. With you by my side, I will seek to deny myself and follow Christ each day. If it pleases God, I pray that he will bless us with children and allow us to raise our children in the love and fear of the Lord. To you I promise my respect, my support, and my prayers. With these vows, I pledge my lifelong faithfulness to you and to God. I surrender our marriage to the Lord as together we seek to glorify him as husband and wife.

Bride: I, _____ (bride), offer myself completely to you, _____ (groom), to be your wife in marriage. Accepting you as a precious and priceless gift from God, I promise to love you unconditionally and to submit to your Christlike leadership in our marriage. I, too, know that I am better able to glorify God with you than apart from you. Next to my relationship to God, my relationship to you is most dear to me. As your wife and accountability partner, I commit to deny myself and follow Christ each day. I pledge to labor by your side as together we grow to love the Lord, our God, with all our heart, soul, mind, and strength. I promise to hold you, to listen to you, to care for you, and to encourage you. In our marriage, I promise to be transparently open with you and to communicate honestly with you. I will work with you in making our home a place of refuge, peace, and comfort. I will seek always to show gentleness and kindness, patience and joy toward you. If it pleases God, I pray that he will bless us with children and allow us to raise our children in the love and fear of the Lord. To you I promise my respect, my support, and my prayers. With these vows, I pledge my life-long faithfulness to you and to God. I surrender our marriage to the Lord as together we seek to glorify him as husband and wife.

THE RING CEREMONY

_____ (groom) and _____ (bride), a wedding ring is a very special and powerful symbol. The rings you exchange today will become outward signs of your vows to Christ and each other, and of your commitment to keep those vows for a lifetime.

_____ (groom), do you give this ring to _____ (bride) as a symbol of a joyful and loving commitment to build a marriage that lasts and as a hallmark of your heart's devotion to her?

Groom responds: "I do."

Then, _____ (groom), place the ring on _____'s (bride's) finger and repeat after me:

Groom: "This ring I give to you as a witness of my vows and of my sacred commitment to you and to Jesus Christ, our Lord and Savior."

_____ (bride), do you give this ring to _____ (groom) as a symbol of a joyful and loving commitment to build a marriage that lasts and as a hallmark of your heart's devotion to him?

Bride responds: "I do."

Then, _____ (bride), place the ring on _____'s (groom's) finger and repeat after me:

Bride: "This ring I give to you as a witness of my vows and of my sacred commitment to you and to Jesus Christ, our Lord and Savior."

THE PRAYER OF CONSECRATION

Father of eternal love, we thank you for this couple, these families, and their lasting love. We thank you for these parents who have raised _____ (groom) and _____ (bride) to love you and to follow you. We thank you for the many years these parents have prayed for their children and for their future mates. We thank you for your faithfulness in answering these prayers and leading _____ (groom) and _____ (bride) to fall in love and now to marry each other. We pray for your continued blessings on these families and on this marriage of their children.

We thank you that we have been privileged to witness with you as _____ (groom) and _____ (bride) have made their vows and exchanged their rings in this holy and sacred hour. By your power and with your blessing, we ask that you empower these two faithfully to keep their vows, to have a love that lasts, successfully to build a marriage that is strong, joyfully to live in your peace, mutually to walk in faith, and confidently to live in your grace. May you receive glory through the marriage of _____ (groom) and _____ (bride). In the name of Jesus we pray. Amen.

THE CANDLE CEREMONY

The candle given by the bride's parents symbolizes the radiance of Christ's love in the lives of _____ (groom) and _____ (bride). The candle given by the groom's parents symbolizes the spiritual growth through the power of the Holy Spirit in their lives. The center candle symbolizes the ruling of God the Father in all of his holiness and splendor in their marriage.

_____ (groom) and _____ (bride), the two outer candles have been lighted by your parents, representing your lives to this moment. They are two distinct lights, each bright and shining on their own. To bring joy and harmony to your home, these two lights must merge into one. This is what the Lord meant when he said, "For this reason a man shall leave his father and mother and be joined to his wife, and the two shall become one" (Matt. 19:5 RSV).

From this time forth, your thoughts shall be for each other rather than your individual selves. Your plans shall be mutual; your joys and sorrows shall be shared alike. _____ (groom) and _____ (bride), take your individual candles and light the center candle to express symbolically the goals of your union: to glorify God in your marriage and to radiate his love to all whose lives you touch. Do not extinguish your individual candles; instead, place them, still lit, in their holders. In doing so, you are symbolizing that, although you are one in union with each other and the Lord, your God-given, individual personalities will still exist and be used by God as his lights in this dark world.

THE SOLO

(To be sung during the lighting of the candles.)

THE PRONOUNCEMENT

_____ (groom) and _____ (bride), you have attested to your belief that God has given you to each other and that you can better glorify God united as husband and wife than as individuals. Today we have come and, with you, worshiped the giver of this unimaginable blessing. Before God and all present, you have confessed your love for each other. You have promised to be faithful to each other and have committed to follow Christ in a lifelong marriage relationship. It is, therefore, my privilege as a minister of the gospel of our Master and Savior to pronounce you husband and wife. What God has joined together in this union, let no person ever attempt to break or destroy.

"And the peace of God, which surpasses all comprehension, shall guard your hearts and your minds in Christ Jesus" (Phil. 4:7, NASB). Amen.

_____ (groom), you may kiss your wife.

THE PRESENTATION OF THE BRIDE AND GROOM

On behalf of the _____ (groom's family), the _____ (bride's family), and the fellowship of faith, I happily introduce to you Mr. and Mrs. _____.

THE RECESSIONAL

Two Are Better than One

THE PRELUDE

(The prelude will consist of the singing and playing of praise choruses and hymns.)

THE PROCESSIONAL

THE CONGREGATIONAL CALL TO PRAISE

We begin this celebration of marriage with a time of prayer and praise. Congregation, as I conclude each sentence of prayer, which is based on the one-hundred-and-forty-fifth psalm, please respond aloud with the phrase, "Praise you, Lord!"

Dear Lord, you are faithful in all your promises.

Congregation responds: "Praise you, Lord!"

You are loving toward all you have made.

Congregation responds: "Praise you, Lord!"

You are near to all who, in truth, call on you.

Congregation responds: "Praise you, Lord!"

You watch over all who love you.

Congregation responds: "Praise you, Lord!"

We praise your name together as we recognize your will at work in bringing _____ (groom) _____ (bride) to this day to become one in Christ.

Congregation responds: "Praise you, Lord!"

(Congregation, you may be seated.)

THE STATEMENT OF MARRIAGE

Hear now these words from the fourth chapter of the Book of Ecclesiastes: "Two are better than one, because they have a good reward for their labor. For if they fall, one will lift up his companion. But woe to him who is alone when he falls, for he has no one to help him up. Again, if two lie down together, they will keep warm; but how can one be warm alone? The one may be overpowered by another, two can withstand him. And a threefold cord is not quickly broken" (vv. 9–12 NKJV).

Jack Benny was a well-known comedian of a recent generation. His longtime friend and partner, George Burns, was interviewed about his relationship with Jack Benny. He said, "Jack and I had a wonderful relationship for nearly fifty-five years. Jack never walked out on me when I sang a song, and I never walked out on him when he played the violin. We laughed together, we played together, we worked together, and we ate together. I suppose that for many of those years we talked every single day."[1]

Every one of us yearns for those kinds of relationships. God made us for companionship, for community, for family, for friendships, for the relationship of husband and wife. When Jesus walked here as God in the flesh, he surrounded himself with followers. He sent them, two by two, to do his work. There is power in unity, when people stand together. That sense of connectedness—of being united for a common cause—brings positive results. It is easy to see why the wisest man who ever lived wrote the words of the passage I just read. Solomon understood the principle that the whole is greater than the sum of its parts. Jesus applied this same principle when he said, "If two of you agree on earth concerning anything that they ask, it will be done for them by My Father in heaven" (Matt. 18:19 NKJV).

The most important relationship one can have is with the One who created us for himself. Our Creator and heavenly Father removes us from our terrible aloneness and brings us into his family, as adopted sons and daughters, with all the family privileges. In doing so, he gives us an eternal, indivisible unity with him. These two, as they make their vows, are uniting as one with each other and one in Christ. Their relationship becomes the kind of relationship to which Solomon referred when he wrote, "A threefold cord is not quickly broken" (Eccl. 4:12*b* NKJV).

THE STATEMENT OF COMMITMENT

_____ (groom) and _____ (bride), do you make a commitment to build a lifetime marriage strengthened by your bond of love for each other and further reinforced by your union in faith with Jesus Christ?

Groom and bride respond: "We do."

THE GIVING OF THE BRIDE

Assured that _____ (groom) and _____ (bride) are ready to affirm their conviction that two are better than one when united as husband and wife in the love of Jesus Christ, I have the privilege to ask, "Who gives this woman to be married to this man?"

Father responds: "Her mother and I."

THE VOWS

_____ (groom) and _____ (bride), please face each other, join hands, and repeat after me:

Groom: "I, _____ (groom), seek with my deepest conviction to become one with you, _____ (bride). I vow to you and to our Lord that my 'I' will become 'we' in the years ahead. I receive you as a gift from God. I will be faithful to you. I will never reject you. I love you without condition, without reservation, and so I promise to love you, to honor you, and never to leave you. In the name of our Savior and Lord, Jesus Christ, I do so promise."

Bride: "I, _____ (bride), seek with my deepest conviction to become one with you, _____ (groom). I vow to you and to our Lord that my 'I' will become 'we' in the years ahead. I receive you as a gift from God. I will be faithful to you. I will never reject you. I love you without condition, without reservation, and so I promise to love you, to honor you, and never to leave you. In the name of our Savior and Lord, Jesus Christ, I do so promise."

THE EXCHANGE OF RINGS

It is easy to see that a ring is a magnificent symbol of oneness. It has been mined from precious elements, purified and blended, and molded into a ribbon of flowing unbrokenness. You will now give these rings to one another as a display of your commitment and of your recognition that you are stronger as two in Christ than you are alone, by yourselves, apart from him and each other.

_____ (groom), take the ring and place it on _____'s (bride's) finger. Repeat these words of love and commitment after me:

Groom: "I, _____ (groom), give this ring to you, _____ (bride), as a symbol of the strength of our love and of our union. From this time forward, we shall no longer be two apart; rather, we are one in Christ. I make this vow in the strong name of Jesus. Amen."

_____ (bride), take the ring and place it on _____'s (groom's) finger. Repeat these words of love and commitment after me:

Bride: "I, _____ (bride), give this ring to you, _____ (groom), as a symbol of the strength of our love and of our union. From this time forward, we shall no longer be two apart; rather, we are one in Christ. I make this vow in the strong name of Jesus. Amen."

THE PRONOUNCEMENT

The Song of Songs reminds us that "my lover is mine and I am his" (Song of Songs 2:16). From this day forward this will be the reality of your lives together as husband and wife. The word *together* will link you and be indicative of the strength of your union that can withstand any attack on your lives or your marriage. Go now in his presence, for he has promised, "I will never leave you nor forsake you" (Josh. 1:5). Yours is a threefold relationship that is forever secure. God bless you, today and always.

I now pronounce and announce that you are husband and wife, Mr. and Mrs. _____.

THE RECESSIONAL

The Promise Keepers

———— ✦ ————

THE PROCESSIONAL
THE INVOCATION

Author of love, Keeper of promises, we have come to this joyous moment with great anticipation. We praise you because you promote joy, you express joy, you *are* joy! At this blessed human event, we are grateful to share the joy of _____ (groom) and _____ (bride). We remember your promise that when "two or three are gathered together in my name, there am I in the midst of them" (Matt. 18:20 KJV), and we invoke your presence now in this place. May you be pleased with that which we do in this sacred hour. May your name be honored. Thank you for all who have been a part of the lives of _____ (groom) and _____ (bride). We recognize in their selfless love and in their investment of time, energy, and resources that they are very much the warp and the woof of the fabric of the two lives that you are weaving together to become one. In the name of the promised One, our Messiah, Jesus Christ, we pray. Amen.

THE STATEMENT OF COMMITMENT

Hear now these words of promise from the New Testament: "The Lord is not slow in keeping his promise" (2 Pet. 3:9). Also, gain assurance from this Old Testament promise: "Not one of all the good promises the LORD your God gave you has failed" (Josh. 23:14). Throughout the Bible, we are reminded that we know, serve, and love a God who always keeps his promise. There is great comfort, reassurance, and power in knowing this truth. It has been said that promise keeping is a powerful means of grace. It is the only way to overcome the unpredictability of the future.

Have you ever given any thought to the fact that only a human can make a promise? No animal can make a promise. No computer or means of technology can promise to be loyal. Only humans can make such a commitment. All human community, from the ghetto to the global village, depends on the power of promising. If we do not keep our promises, we have helped abolish community. Promise making is the social bond that defines who we are in our life together.

Today, you two are making a promise. In marriage your trust is being placed in the commitment and promise given by this person standing next to you. It is the promise that this person will stick with you, no matter what. It is a promise that this person will always be the one person on whom you can depend for anything you need. It is the promise that this person will be a small sanctuary of trust and confidence. When you, _____ (bride), make this promise, you offer your hand in creating a haven of predictable reality in the unpredictable circumstances of tomorrow. When you, _____ (groom), make your promise, you create an island of certainty in a heaving ocean of uncertainty. When you make and keep promises, you most reflect your Savior and Lord, Emmanuel, whose name is, "I am he who will be there with you" (Matt. 1:23, paraphrased). Among all the dimensions of the mature person in Christ, none comes closer to the character of our Lord than the person who dares to make a promise and who has the courage to keep the promises made.[1]

THE GIVING OF THE BRIDE

Believing that you two are ready to enter into the promise keeping of vows that commit you to a life of togetherness, it is my privilege and honor to ask, "Who gives this woman to be married to this man?"

Father responds: "Her mother and I."

THE VOWS

I ask you, _____ (groom) and _____ (bride), to join hands, and for you, _____ (groom) to repeat your vows of promise to _____ (bride).

Groom: "I, _____ (groom), promise you, _____ (bride), that I will cherish you all of my life. I will seek to meet your emotional, physical, and spiritual needs in every way possible. I will be faithful to you above all others. I will seek to demonstrate the love of Christ to you. All I have or ever hope to have, I give to you as my life partner. I receive you as my mate, a special gift from God. I promise to keep my promises, in the name of the promised One, the Messiah."

Will you, _____ (bride), repeat your vows of promise to _____ (groom)?

Bride: "I, _____ (bride), promise you, _____ (groom), that I will cherish you all of my life. I will seek to meet your emotional, physical, and spiritual needs in every way possible. I will be faithful to you above all others. I will seek to demonstrate the love of Christ to you. All I have or ever hope to have, I give to you as my life partner. I receive you as my mate, a special gift from God. I promise to keep my promises, in the name of the promised One, the Messiah."

THE EXCHANGE OF RINGS

These rings you are about to exchange will be the public symbol of your becoming one. They are circles signifying the unity and the eternal nature of Christian love. The placing of these rings on your fingers becomes the seal of the promises you made in Jesus' name.

_____ (groom), take this ring and place it on _____'s (bride's) finger and respond "I will" if this you promise: _____ (bride), I promise you, by the power of Christ's Spirit, that I will keep my vows of promise made at this altar and in the altar of my heart. So help me, God.

Groom responds: "I will."

_____ (bride), take this ring and place it on _____'s (groom's) finger and respond, "I will" if this you promise: _____ (groom), I promise you, by the power of Christ's Spirit, that I will keep my vows of promise made at this altar and in the altar of my heart. So help me, God.

Bride responds: "I will."

THE PRAYER OF DEDICATION

Dear Father and Lord, Promise Giver, Promise Keeper, you have heard the promises made before you, family, and friends. Witness these words of commitment, and give courage, strength, and joy in fulfilling the awesome power of these heavenly promises. To your glory and to the building of a beautiful life of promise keeping, we ask these things in Jesus' name. Amen.

THE PRONOUNCEMENT

It has been said that true love is the ripe fruit of a lifetime.[2] As you keep the promises you have made here today, may your life together bear much love. Believing you both intend to honor and keep your vows, it is my privilege to pronounce you husband and wife. We send you on your way with our prayers that your union will always be filled with true love and blessed by promise keeping. _____ (groom), you may kiss your bride.

I am happy to introduce you to Mr. and Mrs. _____. God bless you now and always.

THE RECESSIONAL

Oneness

———— ❧ ————

THE PROCESSIONAL

THE WELCOME

Hear the words of the psalmist: "Enter his gates with thanksgiving and his courts with praise; give thanks to him and praise his name. For the LORD is good and his love endures forever" (Ps. 100:4–5). We echo these words on this blessed day in the lives of _____ (groom), _____ (bride), and their loved ones.

THE GIVING OF THE BRIDE

It has been said that marriage is the most persistent reminder of the presence of other people, beyond ourselves, in the world. To be married is to be intimately confronted day after day with the mystery of life, with another life outside of oneself.[1] _____ (groom) and _____ (bride) are ready to take this step into the mystery of marriage, of life beyond themselves. With this commitment in mind, it is my pleasure to ask, "Who gives this woman to this man to begin this journey of becoming one in Christ?"

Father responds: "Her mother and I."

THE INVOCATION

Dear holy One, our triune God, we bow before you with the keen awareness that your ways are not our ways and your thoughts are not our thoughts. We recognize that when it comes to marriage you employ new laws of mathematics. It is amazing to us that when two people marry, you formulate a new equation: one plus one equals one. We pray for these two who are committed to seeing that this equation becomes a reality in their lives. Thank you that we can be witnesses with them of your genius in making their marriage add up to oneness with each other and oneness with you. In the name of Jesus Christ, the one true and living Savior. Amen.

THE TEACHING ON MARRIAGE ONENESS

When Jesus walked among men, he taught his followers about oneness in marriage, saying, "In the original creation, God made male and female to be together. Because of this, a man leaves father and mother, and in marriage he becomes one flesh with a woman—no longer two individuals, but forming a new unity. Because God created this organic union of the two sexes, no one should desecrate his art by cutting them apart" (Mark 10:6–9 TMNT). Husband and wife becoming one is not a myth, but surely it is a miracle. It could be compared to the creation of water through the process of combining hydrogen and oxygen—colorless, odorless gases—and passing an electrical charge through these two elements to form a water molecule. In fusing these two substances, a totally new entity is created. While this new entity is made exclusively of the other two, it far exceeds the sum of the parts of the two.

In the same way, when God unites the bride and groom, he takes all their qualities and fuses them into a new entity. He takes the best and the worst of both individuals—the strengths and the weaknesses of both persons—and fuses these into one new entity, so that they might be mutually complementary and encompassing. This process requires adjustment and commitment, but in God's eyes the process of two becoming one is a lifetime relationship begun at marriage.

As the two marriage partners surrender and fuse their bodies in physical union, they have surrendered and fused themselves—for richer, for poorer, in sickness, in health, till death do them part. And God is pleased to seal this union of two becoming one.[2] A poet expressed it beautifully in these words:

> "Melt down two pasts into a single now,
> adventurers, and give each other nerve
> to risk two futures on a single vow . . .
>
> Love is its own invention: all your how
> lies in your singlemindedness to serve,
> to risk two futures on a single vow.
>
> And love is its own discipline: allows
> each lover still a present-self, preserved
> though two pasts melt into a single now . . .
>
> Adventurers have cares, and on your brows
> let all care by your comrade be observed.
> Melt down two pasts into a single now
> and gladly risk two futures on one vow."[3]

THE VOWS

_____ (groom) and _____ (bride), will you face each other? _____ (groom), repeat after me this vow made to _____ (bride):

Groom: "I, _____ (groom), love you, _____ (bride), and am committed to giving my life to be one with yours. I will cleave to you in an unbreakable bond. I will live with you as one in Christ's love. I surrender to you—and for you—my mind, my will, my spirit, my emotions, and all I possess. One will be our indivisible number until death parts us. You can be confident of this promise I make."

_____ (bride), repeat after me this vow made to _____ (groom):

Bride: "I, _____ (bride), love you, _____ (groom), and am committed to giving my life, to be one with yours. I will cleave to you in an unbreakable bond. I will live with you as one in Christ's love. I surrender to you—and for you—my mind, my will, my spirit, my emotions, and all I possess. One will be our indivisible number until death parts us. You can be confident of this promise I make."

THE EXCHANGE OF RINGS

Believing that it is God's will for you two to become one, you will attest this holy vow by the giving of rings which portray the permanence of your union as one.

_____ (groom), place the ring on _____'s (bride's) finger and repeat after me:

Groom: "I, _____ (groom), give you, _____ (bride), this cherished ring as a symbol of our oneness from this day forward. Without you I am only half a person. With you, I am one. In Christ, we are an invincible alliance of love. Our union is stronger than anything we will face together in life."

_____ (bride), place the ring on _____'s (groom's) finger and repeat after me this vow:

Bride: "I, _____ (bride), give you, _____ (groom), this cherished ring as a symbol of our oneness from this day forward. Without you I am only half a person. With you, I am one. In Christ, we are an invincible alliance of love. Our union is stronger than anything we will face together in life."

THE PRONOUNCEMENT

_____ (groom) and _____ (bride), today you begin the task of becoming one. Remember, it is not a quick sprint, but a marathon. At times you will want to give up, but never give up. Keep going. At times you may feel you are running out of energy to continue, but that is better than running away. Marriage, in the long run, is living with the glorious mystery of oneness and facing life's blessings and challenges together. As your oneness grows, so will your bond grow ever closer to the One who binds you to himself with the cords of eternal love. It is in the name of the One who truly unites you in marriage, Jesus Christ, that I pronounce that you are now husband and wife. Let the oneness begin!

THE RECESSIONAL

A Love Song

———— ❧ ————

THE PRELUDE

THE PROCESSIONAL

THE WELCOME

Dear bride and groom, parents, family, and friends, we have come together for a celebration of devotion and love called *marriage*. A marriage is not the *joining* of two worlds; rather, it is the *abandoning* of two worlds, in order that one new world might be formed.[1] We welcome all who witness this sacred union, for weddings are an important part of God's grand design for man's fulfillment and happiness. When God walked among us as Jesus Christ, he performed his first miracle at a wedding in the little village of Cana (John 2:1–11). His presence at the wedding indicates that he did not shun such blessed events; his miracle of changing the water into wine indicates that, in fact, he blessed such events. May we all have a keen awareness of his presence at this wedding today.

THE INVOCATION

Author of love, you promised that where two or three come together in your name, you will be there. Believing your loving promise, we unashamedly welcome you here as our honored guest today! We ask that you once again visit a wedding—this wedding—and, likewise, favor us with your presence, your provision, your power, and your peace. We praise you now and always for your grace and love. Amen.

THE GIVING OF THE BRIDE

Marriage is a very special gift to the world. It is God's ideal mechanism for stretching us to reach our highest potential. The marriage ceremony is not a magic wand that removes the complexities of personality and background, but it serves as an instrument to maximize the best parts of two individuals while changing them into one. There is an old proverb that says, "A thousand-mile journey begins with the first steps." With this in mind, let this journey of marriage begin by taking a first important step, a step of separation away from parental control and provision and a step toward your two independent lives being merged into one. "Who gives this woman to be married to this man?"

Father responds: "I do."

THE WORDS OF LOVE

_____ (groom) and _____ (bride), two songs of love found in the Bible are world famous, because of their timelessness, power, inspiration, and scope. They soar with an eloquence rarely duplicated in literature or poetry. The first love song, found in 1 Corinthians, chapter 13, has been used to define true love over the centuries. _____ (groom) and _____ (bride), listen carefully and let God's Word guide you now as you enter the marriage relationship.

"If I speak with human eloquence and angelic ecstasy but don't love, I'm nothing but the creaking of a rusty gate. If I speak God's Word with power, revealing all his mysteries and making everything plain as day, and if I have faith that says to a mountain, 'Jump,' and it jumps, but I don't have love, I'm nothing. If I give everything I own to the poor and even go to the stake to be burned as a martyr, but I don't love, I've gotten nowhere. So, no matter what I say, what I believe, and what I do, I'm bankrupt without love.

> Love never gives up.
> Love cares more for others than for self.
> Love doesn't want what it doesn't have.
> Love doesn't strut,
> Doesn't have a swelled head,
> Doesn't force itself on others,
> Isn't always 'me first,'
> Doesn't fly off the handle,
> Doesn't keep score of the sins of others,
> Doesn't revel when others grovel,
> Takes pleasure in the flowering of truth,
> Puts up with anything,
> Trusts God always,
> Always looks for the best,
> Never looks back,
> But keeps going to the end . . .

We don't yet see things clearly. We're squinting in a fog, peering through a mist. But it won't be long before the weather clears and the sun shines bright! We'll see it all then, see it all as clearly as God sees us, knowing him directly just as he knows us! But for right now, until that completeness, we have three things to do to lead us toward that consummation: Trust steadily in God, hope unswervingly, love extravagantly. And the best of the three is love" (1 Cor. 13:1–7, 12–13, TMNT).

_____ (groom) and _____ (bride), you have heard love beautifully defined. Listen now to the lyrics of a second love song, found in the eighth chapter of the Song of Songs, that also sings of love in action: "Place me like a seal over your heart, like a seal on your arm; for love is as strong as death, its jealousy unyielding as the grave. It burns like blazing fire, like a mighty flame. Many waters cannot quench love; rivers cannot wash it away. If one were to give all the wealth of his house for love, it would be utterly scorned" (Song of Songs 8:6–7).

_____ (groom) and _____ (bride), the second love song exalts four qualities of love that you would be wise to embrace in your marriage:

Love is inescapable. The love song says that true "love is as strong as death . . . unyielding as the grave" (v. 6*b*). Love is as *inescapable* as death. It has an unshakable quality. Like death, it is unyielding. We know that death is the inescapable consequence of sin. We know also that God's love is greater than death, because his love conquered death through Christ's resurrection. It is amazing that human love has that sort of capacity!

Love is intense. In fact, true love is as *intense* as fire. "It burns like blazing fire, like a mighty flame" (v. 6*c*). How hot is fire? Scientists have estimated that the core of the sun carries a temperature of approximately 27,000,000 degrees F. Love, burning with that intensity, goes beyond today's mind-set which says, *"I will stay with you, so long as I love you."* Marriage built on a biblically intense union is more than a contract, more than a device to meet the needs of two adults, more than an instant family. It is two individuals united and committed at the deepest, most intense level.

Love is invincible. True love is so *invincible* that it cannot be overwhelmed by life's devastating floods. "Many waters cannot quench love; rivers cannot wash it away" (v.7*a*). Mature marriage partners are realistic in their understanding that their mate is not perfect, nor are they themselves perfect. Together, in love, they must work through differences in social, spiritual, familial, and educational backgrounds. They also must adjust to personality differences. All of this takes genuine love. This kind of love grows until it becomes so strong that it is invincible. We see an invincible love portrayed in the movie *Shadowlands,* when Joy Gresham reminds C. S. Lewis that their joy would soon end, for she was about to die. Lewis replies that he doesn't want to think about it. At this Joy responds, "The pain is part of the happiness. That's the deal." Lewis stayed with Joy until cancer took her in death. That is invincible love.

Love is invaluable. "If one were to give all the wealth of his house for love, it would be utterly scorned" (v.7b). You can't buy something that is priceless. A husband of more than fifty years was asked if fifty years weren't a long time to be married to one person. To this he replied, "It would have been a lot longer without her."[2] While there is no way to estimate the value of true love, we do know that it grows exponentially in value over the years.

The kind of love described in these poignant love songs is not a worldly love or a natural love; rather, this enduring kind of love is a supernatural love. From what source does this love come? The Bible says, "Let us love one another, for love comes from God" (1 John 4:7). _____ (groom) and _____ (bride), loving each other can be difficult at times, especially if you trust in the world's advice about how to love. Instead, model the love that was described in these two love songs from God's Word. Today and always, let your love for each other come from God.

THE VOWS

The taking of vows is an act of faith and commitment. If we were faithful by nature, vows would not be necessary. Because we are neither inherently faithful nor honest, we must stand up and declare our commitment to each other before God and man. We declare our vows with the witness and support of family and friends. We also declare our absolute dependence upon God's resources, which are utterly beyond human strength. Our marriage vows give glory to God, for it is only God's grace that enables such love and commitment to exist.[3] Believing you both, as true children of the living God, seek God's resources of love and commitment, I now ask that you face each other and pledge your vows with the desire of writing your own love song in marriage.

_____ (groom), repeat after me:

Groom: "I, _____ (groom), having received the gift of God's love and grace in my life, do commit my love to you, _____ (bride). I will seek to love you with an unselfish love that will never give up, an abiding commitment that will never break, and an unspeakable joy that will grow for as long as we both shall live."

_____ (bride), repeat after me:

Bride: "I, _____ (bride), having received the gift of God's love and grace in my life, do commit my love to you, _____ (groom). I will seek to love you with an unselfish love that will never give up, an abiding commitment that will never break, and an unspeakable joy that will grow for as long as we both shall live."

THE RINGS

The rings you exchange are symbols of the love and vows you have promised to each other before God and witnesses. As you wear these symbols, may they remind you of your love for each other and your desire that your love be a deep and lasting reflection of God's love for you.

_____ (groom), place this symbol of true love on _____'s (bride's) finger and repeat after me:

Groom: "_____ (bride), I give you this ring as a holy witness of my love and of my trust in our God to be our provision, our protection, our power, and our peace. I will love you forever, for my love is of Christ."

_____ (bride), place this symbol of true love on _____'s (groom's) finger and repeat after me:

Bride: "_____ (groom), I give you this ring as a holy witness of my love and of my trust in our God to be our provision, our protection, our power, and our peace. I will love you forever, for my love is of Christ."

THE SONG AND PRAYER OF CONSECRATION

(The couple will kneel in prayer as the song begins. They will remain kneeling throughout the song and the prayer of consecration.)

The Greatest of These Is Love

Father of faith and forever love, we come now to ask you to seal these words and intentions of _____ (groom) and _____ (bride). May they be encouraged to know that in a world where faithfulness is rare, you are ever faithful and able to give the strength to mean and keep these vows. May the memories of these minutes always bring joy. May the vows always bring renewal. May the rings always bring reflection upon a love ever growing. May their marriage always be a reminder of your eternal love that never grows faint and of your everlasting vow to keep us unto yourself even beyond death. In the name of the Father, Son, and Holy Spirit. Amen.

(The couple will stand at the conclusion of the prayer.)

THE UNITY CANDLE

Before you are three candles. The two outer candles represent your individual lives. You both were born into families who understood and embraced God's love and grace. Your parents raised you as children of the heavenly Father. Now, as adults, as marriage partners, it is time for you to establish your own home, your family of faith. As you together light the center candle to signify your oneness in joining as partners in marriage and your uniting to glorify God in and through your love song of marriage, do not extinguish your individual candles. God, who created you in his image, also created you to be unique in your personality, abilities, and potential for touching other lives. Let the One who is called "the Light of the World" shine in and through you both in your lives and in your marriage—today and always.

(The couple will light the unity candle as the song is sung.)

THE SONG OF UNITY

You Are the Light

THE BENEDICTION

"May our Lord Jesus Christ himself and God our Father, who loved us and by his grace gave us eternal encouragement and good hope, encourage your hearts and strengthen you in every good deed and word" (2 Thess. 2:16–17). Amen.

THE PRONOUNCEMENT

_____ (groom) and _____ (bride), thank you for the privilege of sharing this unforgettable moment in your lives. As you have made your vows, given to each other beautiful tokens of those vows, and heard the challenge from God's Word to establish your marriage upon God's defining love, we have been reminded of a love that finds its security and significance in God's promise that "neither death, nor life, nor angels, nor principalities, nor powers, nor things present, nor things to come, nor height, nor depth, nor any other creature, shall be able to separate us from the love of God, which is in Christ Jesus our Lord" (Rom. 8:38–39, KJV). _____ (groom) and _____ (bride), live your married lives in the reality of his promises.

And now it is a joy to pronounce that from this day forward you are husband and wife, and to introduce you as Mr. and Mrs. _____. _____ (groom), you may kiss your bride. Go now in the love and grace of our Lord and Savior, Jesus Christ.

THE RECESSIONAL

THE POSTLUDE

The Power of Words

———— ❧ ————

THE PRELUDE

THE PROCESSIONAL

THE CALL TO WORSHIP

Congregation, would you join me in repeating these wonderful words of assurance? "This is the day the LORD has made, let us rejoice and be glad in it" (Ps. 118:24).

THE INVOCATION

Word of God, we praise you for the wonderful words of life which have opened our ears to hear your voice, opened our hearts to receive your grace, and opened our eyes to behold your glory. We realize that without your Word, we would be unable to know the full joy of a wedding day in your presence or a marriage under your control. We pray that the words we speak today will be words of truth, words of love, words of devotion, words of praise. Like Isaiah, we, too, realize we are

167

people of unclean lips (Isa. 6:5). Touch us and enable us to glorify you in all we say and do in this sacred hour. We will be careful to give you all the praise. In the name of the author and perfecter of our praise. Amen.

THE GIVING OF THE BRIDE

_____ (groom) and _____ (bride), much prayer, love, guidance, and sacrifice have gone into preparing you for this transitional experience in your life. I know that you are grateful to God for your parents, grandparents, family members, and friends who have given you the gift of themselves. You have indicated that you are ready to begin a new chapter in your life; so I ask, "Who gives _____ (bride) to be married to _____ (groom) as they enter into this new relationship of Christian marriage?"

Father responds: "I do," or "Her mother and I do."

THE WORDS ON MARRIAGE

If asked, "What is the single most important ingredient of a successful marriage?" most people would probably say that it is love. There is another ingredient, however, which must precede love and is necessary for love—and that is trust. Love always blossoms out of trust. How does a couple develop trust? Trust grows when a couple learns to communicate openly, honestly, vulnerably, and intimately with each other. Communication, then, is a third important ingredient for a successful marriage. It has been said, "Before I can love you, I must get to know you, and before I get to know you, I must be able to communicate with you."[1]

_____ (groom) and _____ (bride), there is great power in the words you speak, especially the words you speak to each other. Learn to communicate with this mate whom you love and with whom you want to grow more in love. Why is good communication such an essential ingredient? It has been frequently documented by marriage counselors and pastors alike that poor communication is responsible for the majority of problems in marriage. Without a doubt, there is power in words!

The Word of God gives us valuable insight and direction concerning the proper use of words. Ephesians 4:15 expresses the art of effective communication: "Speaking the truth in love, we will in all things grow up into him who is the Head, that is, Christ." This is no easy task! You may recall that the right hemisphere of the brain controls the emotions, feelings, creativity, and artistic impulses, while the left hemisphere of the brain controls the logical, analytical aspects of behavior. By our very nature, women generally tend to be more right-brained in their orientation and men generally tend to be more left-brained in theirs. Thinking more globally, intuitively, and relationally, women tend to be more gifted communicators. Men, on the other hand, tend to think more linearly and communicate more succinctly.[2] The result is that men tend to say only what they mean and women tend to say more than they mean.

How does this impact marriages? Wives tend to believe their husbands are not saying everything they mean, while husbands tend to believe that their wives mean everything they say.[3] How can husbands and wives better communicate? Someone has suggested that effective communication is only accomplished through "the meeting of meaning." That is, effective marital communication occurs when—and only when—your meaning meets your mate's meaning across the bridge of words, tones, deeds, and actions, and when understanding occurs.[4]

It has been said that if you don't communicate you will disintegrate.[5] What are some of the barriers to effective marital communication? Some communication barriers are: anger, tears, silence, criticism, frustration, and failure to listen. How, then, do you build lines of communication in your marriage instead of walls of silence? The apostle Paul comes to our assistance when he writes, "Do not let any unwholesome talk come out of your mouths, but only what is helpful for building others up according to their needs, that it may benefit those who listen" (Eph. 4:29). With this biblical goal of building up your mate according to their needs, you can mature as communicators by: being a good listener, saying what you mean and meaning what you say, tackling problems and not each other, encouraging much, and praying aloud together.

It has been said that the five most important words are: "I am proud of you." The four most important words are: "What is your opinion?" The three most important words are "if you please." The two most important words are "thank you." And the least important word is "I."[6] There are two other golden expressions that will wear well through the years: "I'm sorry" (because as sinners, we will sin against our mate) and "I love you" (because you will never get tired of hearing it and you should never get tired of saying it). These choice words are what the writer of Proverbs calls "apples of gold in settings of silver" (Prov. 25:11). Without a doubt, communication is an essential ingredient in a successful marriage.

THE VOWS

_____ (groom) and _____ (bride), recognizing that there *is* power in your words, are you ready to speak words of lifetime commitment to each other?

Groom and bride respond: "We are."

Then, _____ (groom), face _____ (bride) and repeat these life-changing words after me:

Groom: "I, _____ (groom), promise you, _____ (bride), and our Lord that I am committed to sharing romance with you, companionship with you, communication with you, and facing life's challenges with you. I promise to support you and to grow in Christ with you all the days of my life. I give you my solemn word and my deepest love."

_____ (bride), now it is your opportunity to repeat these life-changing words after me:

Bride: "I, _____ (bride), promise you, _____ (groom), and our Lord that I am committed to sharing romance with you, companionship with you, communication with you, and facing life's challenges with you. I promise to support you and to grow in Christ with you all the days of my life. I give you my solemn word and my deepest love."

THE RINGS

_____ (groom) and _____ (bride), you have spoken powerful words of commitment to each other. Are you ready now to seal those vows with a symbol of your love and commitment?

Groom and bride respond: "We are."

_____ (groom), do you have a ring?

Groom responds: "I do." (The best man gives the ring to the groom, who then places the ring on the minister's Bible.)

_____ (groom), take this ring, place it on _____'s (bride's) finger, and repeat after me:

Groom: "With all the commitment of my heart, I give you this cherished ring. It is yours to serve as a visible reminder of the words I have spoken in reverent promise to you and to God this day. These words I have spoken in truth and in the name of the Father, the Son, and the Holy Spirit. Amen."

_____ (bride), do you have a ring?

Bride responds: "I do." (The maid or matron of honor gives the ring to the bride, who then places the ring on the minister's Bible.)

_____ (bride), take this ring, place it on _____'s (groom's) finger, and repeat after me:

Bride: "With all the commitment of my heart, I give you this cherished ring. It is yours to serve as a visible reminder of the words I have spoken in reverent promise to you and to God this day. These words I have spoken in truth and in the name of the Father, the Son, and the Holy Spirit. Amen."

THE BENEDICTION

Father, your Word is eternal. Your Word is a lamp to our feet and a light to our path. The Word you speak is good. You are the living Word. Your Word is the saving Word. Your Word is the Word of life. You have reminded us that it is better not to make a vow than to make a vow and not fulfill it. We ask your divine assistance in helping this couple keep their words of promise. We pray these things in the name of the Word of Life, Jesus Christ, our Lord. Amen.

THE PRONOUNCEMENT

In the light of your vows here spoken and promised, and with our fervent prayers that you will keep your words, it is my honor to pronounce you husband and wife, Mr. and Mrs. _____. Now may the Word of blessing follow you all the days of your lives.

THE RECESSIONAL

A Marriage Made in Heaven

--- ❧ ---

THE PROCESSIONAL

THE WELCOME

On behalf of _____ (groom), _____ (bride), and their families, it is my joyful privilege to welcome you to this ceremony of marriage. Today, while we will naturally focus on the love and commitment of this couple, we will also focus on the deep love of God, his commitment to care for his own, and his faithfulness in fulfilling his commitment to his children. _____ (groom) and _____ (bride), believing that their heavenly Father brought them together in a relationship to fulfill his purpose of their being united in marriage, stand before you with an overwhelming sense of gratitude to their Lord for what he is doing in their lives. They truly believe that theirs is a marriage made in heaven!

THE LORD'S PRAYER

As I pray, please silently pray with me: *Our Father which art in heaven, Hallowed be thy name!* We worship you, God of heaven and earth, as the only true and living God. As your adopted children, we bow gratefully in obedience before you. *Thy kingdom come. Thy will be done in earth, as it is in heaven.* We praise you for the plan that you have for each of our lives. You have been good to lead _____ (groom) and _____ (bride) to understand that your plan for their lives includes their being united in marriage. They desire to do your will more than their own. *Give us this day our daily bread.* We thank you that you are the One who provides for our needs and who will provide for the needs of _____ (groom) and _____ (bride). You are truly a good and faithful Master.

And forgive us our debts, as we forgive our debtors. We bless you for the great love and mercy you have extended to us in our salvation. As you have forgiven us our debts, we ask that you teach _____ (groom) and _____ (bride) your lessons of love and forgiveness in their relationship with each other throughout all the years of their marriage. *And lead us not into temptation, but deliver us from evil.* In the same way, we ask your protection over this marriage. Keep _____ (groom) and _____ (bride) faithful in their commitment to each other and to you. *For thine is the kingdom, and the power, and the glory, for ever. Amen* (Matt. 6:9–13, KJV).

THE GIVING OF THE BRIDE

Choosing a partner for life is a daunting challenge. Someone has said, "Make the choice of a marital partner carefully and prayerfully, as you are playing for keeps."[1] In a time when 50 percent of all marriages end in divorce (and with half of those disintegrating within three years and most of those dissolving within seven years);[2] yet, you both optimistically approach this day, believing that it is God's will for you to be husband and wife. It has been obvious that you both are determined that your marriage will be one of permanence. You are persuaded that marriage is a divine concept, conceived in the very heart of God.

With confidence that it is God's plan for you to succeed in your desire to be one in Christ and that what he wills, he will bless, it is my privilege to ask, "Who gives _____ (bride) to be married to _____ (groom)?"

Father responds: "Her mother and I give her in marriage, asking the Lord's richest blessings on this union."

THE MEANING OF A MARRIAGE MADE IN HEAVEN

Marriage is God's idea, not the invention of a clever sociologist who thought it would be a good way to organize humanity.[3] The first wedding is recorded in Genesis, chapter 2: God saw it was "not good for the man to be alone" (v. 18). What, then, is the meaning and the power of a marriage made in heaven?

A marriage made in heaven gives one perfect companionship. "The LORD God said, 'It is not good for the man to be alone'" (Gen. 2:18). Adam—in a perfect environment, in a perfect relationship with God—realized that in creation he saw corresponding creatures: for the tiger, a tigress; for the bull, a cow; for the lion, a lioness. For man, however, there was no correspondence in being to him. Adam was alone. A famous actress once told some friends that the thing in life she most desired was marriage. They asked why—when she had everything: fame, close friends, social life, possessions. This actress replied, "I want so desperately to have someone to nudge."[4] We all can relate to how she felt. We well understand that it is not good to be alone.

A marriage made in heaven gives one a helper for life. "For Adam no suitable helper was found" (Gen. 2:20). A helper is not a hindrance but a counterpart—one who completes the other. Each married partner must never forget that the other is not a beast of burden to be used or abused. When this happens, one will destroy the other by neglect and misunderstanding. Rather, a helper is to be cherished and respected. Of the twenty-one appearances of the word *helper* in the Old Testament, fifteen refer to God as the *helper* of humanity—the One who assists the desperate and the helpless. As the human needs the divine, so man cannot exist without woman.[5] He needs a helper.

A marriage made in heaven gives a person an appreciation for the goodness and blessing of God's gift. "Then the LORD God made a woman from the rib he had taken out of the man, and he brought her to the man. The man said, 'This is now bone of my bones and flesh of my flesh; she shall be called "woman," for she was taken out of man'" (Gen. 2:22–23). Also, we read: "So God created man in his own image, in the image of God he created him; male and female he created them . . . God saw all that he had made, and it was very good" (Gen. 1:27, 31a). Man—created as male and female beings—was made in the image of God. God declared his creations to be *very* good. Female, made from the rib of the male, was truly God's amazing construction project— some say the apex of all creation. She was God's good gift to man. In this wonderful creative act, God displayed in woman the absolute unity and dignity of the human race.[6] In a marriage made in heaven, the couple understands more fully the purpose, the goodness, and the joy of God's creating a mate in his image and for each other.

A marriage made in heaven gives perseverance. "For this reason a man will leave his father and mother and be united to his wife" (Gen. 2:24a). "To leave" reminds us of the principle of severance. It means "to forsake or to abandon." It is an attitude, not necessarily a geographical change. It does not mean to snub the parents. In marriage, one moves from a relationship of obedience to the parents to a relationship of honor with the parents. "To be united," or, as some say, "to cleave," reflects the principle of permanence.[7] It means "to stick like glue." It's the kind of permanence a man displayed while standing by his dying wife day after day. One day when the husband had been attending his wife for hours one day, a concerned friend remarked, "You've been here a long time. Don't you need to leave and get some rest?" To this the husband responded, "What are a few hours or a few days, when she's given me thirty-nine years?"

A marriage made in heaven gives oneness. "And they will become one flesh" (Gen. 2:24b). In God's eyes, a unique bond takes place when a man and woman join in sexual union. That is one important reason why marriage vows are not to be broken by infidelity. This oneness in marital relations is compared to the Christian conversion experience, for in the moment when a person is born again in Jesus Christ, that person becomes one with Christ in a union that grows until the process is ultimately consummated in heaven.[8]

THE VOWS

_____ (groom) and _____ (bride), please turn and face each other.

_____ (groom), will you repeat after me this vow made to _____ (bride)?

Groom: "I receive you, _____ (bride), as a gift from God. I promise to you today, and for as long as we shall live, that I will be your companion. I will be your helpmate. I will be one with you and with you alone. I will establish our marriage as a permanent commitment so long as we are one in Jesus Christ."

_____ (bride), will you repeat after me this vow made to _____ (groom)?

Bride: "I receive you, _____ (groom), as a gift from God. I promise to you today, and for as long as we shall live, that I will be your companion. I will be your helpmate. I will be one with you and with you alone. I will establish our marriage as a permanent commitment so long as we are one in Jesus Christ."

THE RINGS

These rings are very special. You carefully selected these rings because they will represent to you and the world your most sacred and cherished human experience: your union in marriage. You will proudly wear these rings, for they symbolize the joy you experience in being united to this one whom you love and cherish. You will also gratefully wear these rings, for they symbolize the grace of God in bringing you both together and in declaring that his plan was too big for one alone— it demanded the union of two.

_____ (groom), repeat after me:

Groom: "I, _____ (groom), joyfully give this ring to you, _____ (bride), as an emblem of my devotion to you, of my promises to you, and of my commitment to you, for as long as God gives us the blessing of life."

_____ (bride), repeat after me:

Bride: "I, _____ (bride), joyfully give this ring to you, _____ (groom), as an emblem of my devotion to you, of my promises to you, and of my commitment to you, for as long as God gives us the blessing of life."

THE BENEDICTION

Our Creator, Sustainer, and Savior, _____ (groom) and _____ (bride) have pledged their commitment to you and to each other. We acknowledge that their future rests in your hands. They offer their oneness to you, as you are the One who binds them together in a union that is not to be broken in life. We pray that you will bless them with a marriage made in heaven and that you will build a marriage that far outlasts the wedding. May your favor rest upon _____ (groom) and _____ (bride) now and always. In the name of Jesus Christ, our Lord. Amen

THE PRONOUNCEMENT

This truly has been a joyful occasion! As you begin your journey together, never forget that marriage is not a 50/50 proposition; rather, it is a 100 percent effort from each of you. The success of your marriage will help many to honor the name and character of our Lord, Jesus Christ. As this becomes a reality, you will find joy and fulfillment.

Convinced that it is your heart's desire to be united in marriage, it is my privilege to pronounce that from this day forward you will be known as husband and wife.

I am happy to introduce you now as Mr. and Mrs. _____ (groom's full name).

THE RECESSIONAL

A Portrait of Our Home

——————— ✢ ———————

THE PRELUDE

THE PROCESSIONAL

THE WELCOME

Oh, the sheer joy of a wedding ceremony! It's that point of time that we will remember by saying, "Here, at this moment, loyalties and authorities changed hands. Things are different now."[1] Today, in this sacred hour, things are changing before our eyes. Just look! Grasp the significance of this moment. We are witnessing a new home being established.

THE INVOCATION

Creator God, Lord of our homes, we are deeply aware of your abiding interest in this marriage and in the families of _____ (groom) and _____ (bride). We cannot go forward without asking you to create in us a profound sense of your presence at this wedding. We thank you that the very idea of marriage and family sprang from your will. We are grateful for your plan to build strong homes that produce strong lives. We recognize that you established two strong pillars for every home: the husband and the wife. You have reminded us in your Word: "Unless the LORD builds the house, its builders labor in vain" (Ps. 127:1). In the confidence that you will build this union into an enduring home, we lift our hearts in praise. We recognize your position as the exalted leader of this home and as the Lord and Savior of _____ (groom) and _____ (bride).

We pray now that as this couple begins their days together as husband and wife, may they be filled with the awareness of the presence of your Spirit. And as they begin to establish their new home, may it be filled with the goodness of your love. We pray these things in the name of the One who is the cornerstone of the home, Jesus Christ. Amen.

THE STATEMENT OF COMMITMENT

Do you, _____ (groom), recognize that God has made marriage the primary relationship of all mankind?

Groom responds: "I do."

Are you ready to commit yourself to _____ (bride) in that relationship for the rest of your life as you establish your home to the glory of God?

Groom responds: "I am."

Do you, _____ (bride), recognize that God has made marriage the primary relationship of all mankind?

Bride responds: "I do."

Are you ready to commit yourself to _____ (groom) in that relationship for the rest of your life as you establish your home to the glory of God?

Bride responds: "I am."

THE GIVING OF THE BRIDE

Believing that both of you are committed to building a marriage on the foundation of a love greater than your own and to establishing a home that will have Jesus Christ as its cornerstone, it is my privilege to ask, "Who gives _____ (bride) to be married to _____ (groom)?"

Father responds: "Her mother and I do."

THE STATEMENT OF MARRIAGE AND HOME

A class of preschoolers was asked to draw a picture of what they wanted to be when they grew up. One little girl was having a tough time getting started. Over and over, the teacher encouraged her to give it a try. The little girl finally explained to the teacher, "I want to be married, but I don't know how to draw it."[2] For many of us, we, too, would have difficulty in drawing a picture of marriage. We probably would attempt to illustrate marriage by drawing a portrait of a home: a house with a husband and wife, probably with some children, and, of course, a picket fence.

How would you draw a marriage? Would you illustrate marriage by drawing a portrait of a home? If so, what then are foundational qualities for a home? The task is not easy, but Scripture can help us with this. There we can find the blueprints for a home. Let us begin with the words of Jesus in the seventh chapter of the Gospel of Matthew. There he speaks of a house built on a rock (v. 24). Jesus points out that when storms came, that house stood the test because it was built on a solid foundation (v. 25). In a time when many marriages and families are being swept away by the destructive winds of a self-indulgent society and of a "me first" mentality, _____ (groom) and _____ (bride), it would be prudent for you to examine the portrait of the home that is a masterpiece of the master artist himself. It will give you a picture of what marriage should look like.

The portrait of an enduring home and marriage should be framed by:

Consecration to Jesus Christ. "'Love the Lord your God with all your passion and prayer and intelligence.' This is the most important, the first on any list" (Matt. 22:37–38 TMNT). *Consecration* means to set apart as holy and separate from the world. _____ (groom) and _____ (bride), now is the time to set apart your marriage and your home as separate from the world. The lifestyle of your marriage and home should reflect a Christian world and life view, which is distinctly different than that of the world. Let serving and pleasing God be the mission of your marriage.

The portrait of a home and a marriage itself is depicted by:

Compassion. Compassion should be expressed in your relationship and in your home. The apostle Peter commanded husbands to "be considerate as you live with your wives" (1 Pet. 3:7). Likewise, wives should do the same. _____ (groom) and _____ (bride), that means that you both are to be considerate of each other, day in and day out. That can be a tough order at those times when you are facing stress or distress, when you or your mate is tired or ill, or when you have to care for children or family members. This, however, is a nonnegotiable. You are always to strive to show Christlike compassion to your mate.

Communication. One of the best predictors of true happiness in marriage and in the home is your mutual ability to listen and to share. _____ (groom) and _____ (bride), do not play games with each other. Always tell the truth, even when it hurts. You can do this without going out of the way to hurt your mate. Love can survive large problems better in the open than small ones buried and smoldering. Thinking together is more important than thinking alike. Communication puts love into action.[3]

Conflict Resolution. Marriage is not a war where you sleep with the enemy. _____ (groom) and _____ (bride), picture yourselves as two people joined together in a foxhole, cooperating in a battle against common enemies which the Bible identifies as the world, the flesh, and the devil. You cannot declare war on your mate and defeat the enemy! As you work through your conflicts, keep in mind the words of Robert Louis Stevenson: "Make the most of the best and the least of the worst."[4]

Commitment. If you keep your vows, your vows will keep you. Understand this well. Separation or divorce should not be considered. You stay together because you want to stay together. It is a knot so tightly tied that it can be unraveled only by death. It is a grip of your hands that never turns loose until heaven becomes your home. Listen to these words of a poet who eloquently paints a verbal picture of hands joined in marital commitment:

> A good marriage is a lifetime of hands.
> It's a shaking hand sliding a shiny gold band onto the finger
>   of another shaking hand . . .
> It's hands touching in sudden tenderness, or swinging together
>   down a crowded street, or fingers interlocking in the darkness
>   of a theater.
> It's expressive hands: the playful pat . . . the beckoning waves . . . the
>   "Help me please" gesture . . .
> It's two ecstatic hands being grasped by tiny brand new hands,
> It's hurrying hands setting dinner for hungry hands . . .
> It's a proud hand introducing an embarrassed hand . . .
> It's healthy hands holding sick hands.
> It's hands joining in prayer.
> And finally, it's a shaking hand sliding a dull gold band off
>   the finger of a very still hand.[5]

THE EXCHANGE OF VOWS

_____ (groom) and _____ (bride), would you face each other, join your hands in love, and repeat after me?

Groom: "I, _____ (groom), promise you, _____ (bride), that I will hold your hands as long as God gives us life. You are an incredible gift from God; and, as such, I receive you as my wife with unspeakable joy and gratitude, just as I received Christ as my Savior. I pledge that I will always seek God's best for you in your life, in our marriage, and in our home. I promise I will join with you in building an enduring home and marriage for the glory of God. I make my vows to you in love and without any reservation."

Bride: "I, _____ (bride), promise you, _____ (groom), that I will hold your hands as long as God gives us life. You are an incredible gift from God; and, as such, I receive you as my husband with unspeakable joy and gratitude, just as I received Christ as my Savior. I pledge that I will always seek God's best for you in your life, in our marriage, and in our home. I promise I will join with you in building an enduring home and marriage for the glory of God. I make my vows to you in love and without any reservation."

THE EXCHANGE OF RINGS

Some people wear rings as a fashion statement. Some wear rings to communicate status. Some wear rings to show wealth. The wedding rings that you are about to wear, however, attest to love and commitment. When you wear this wedding ring, you will be telling the world, "I am committed to my mate. I have pledged my love and faithfulness to my mate for the rest of our lives together; and, likewise, my mate has done the same. We are committed to building a strong marriage and home. I wear this ring proudly as a symbol of our love and affection."

_____ (groom), does this reflect your heart as you give this ring to _____ (bride)?

Groom responds: "Yes, it does."

Then, _____ (groom), as you hold the hand of _____ (bride), place this ring on her finger and repeat these words of commitment after me:

Groom: "I, _____ (groom), give this ring to you, _____ (bride), as a seal of the vows I have spoken. Let it be a symbol to all others that nothing will be permitted to loosen our grip in marriage. I give it to you as witness of my love for you and of my promises to God."

_____ (bride), does this, likewise, reflect your heart as you give this ring to _____ (groom)?

Bride responds: "Yes, it does."

Then, _____ (bride), as you hold the hand of _____ (groom), place this ring on his finger and repeat these words of commitment after me:

Bride: "I, _____ (bride), give this ring to you, _____ (groom), as a seal of the vows I have spoken. Let it be a symbol to all others that nothing will be permitted to loosen our grip in marriage. I give it to you as witness of my love for you and of my promises to God."

THE SONG AND PRAYER OF DEDICATION

(The couple will kneel at the kneeling bench as the song begins. They will remain kneeling throughout the song and throughout the prayer of dedication.)

Dear Lord and Master of the home, hear our prayer for _____ (groom) and _____ (bride) as these two establish their marriage and their home. May their love never become unraveled or stripped of its splendor; rather, may it grow as enduring and as powerful as your love for us. Through their love for you and each other, build a marriage and a home that will stand the test of time. We pray these things in the name of the One who builds forever, Jesus Christ. Amen.

THE PRONOUNCEMENT

You have given your words of testimony as well as your vows of love and commitment. Now, by the authority of the laws of this state, by the communion and blessing of the triune God, I, as the Lord's minister, do declare that God has joined you together as husband and wife.

THE RECESSIONAL

PART 3

Appendices

———— ✌ ————

Wedding Guidelines

—————— ⚬❦⚬ ——————

1. Only Christian marriages will be performed at our church. Both parties are to be committed to Christ and to the principles of Christian marriage. If one or both parties are not Christians and come to a conference with a staff pastor, every effort will be made to lead them to a saving knowledge of Jesus Christ.

2. All couples (members and nonmembers) desiring to be married at our church will be instructed to attend preparation-for-marriage classes. Any alternate plan must be worked out with the assistant pastor.

3. If a couple is denied marriage by any pastor of our church for any reason, the pastor asked to perform the ceremony will report it to the pastoral staff at their next scheduled staff meeting.

4. If a "denied" couple requests another pastor of our church to marry them, no decision can be made until the two pastors have discussed the circumstances together.

5. A couple must have been dating for a minimum of six months prior to the wedding date in order to be married at our church.

6. No remarriages after divorce will be performed until at least one year has passed from the finalization of the divorce.

7. Our church's wedding policy manual, *The Wedding Handbook,* will serve as the guidelines for use of the facilities, for scheduling the wedding, for selecting music, etc.

8. No wedding will be calendared until the couple has a conference with the staff pastor chosen to perform the ceremony.

9. Because of the high volume of demands for the facilities of our church, members of the church and/or their immediate families have first choice in using the facilities.

10. Nonmembers may use the facilities of our church for weddings upon the approval of the appropriate staff member. The date of such weddings, however, will not be placed on the church calendar more than four months in advance.

11. Ministers other than our church staff pastors may participate in weddings held at the church only after receiving approval by the assistant pastor. A letter outlining intentions for counseling and service planning must be sent from that minister to our assistant pastor. The scheduled wedding date is tentative until this process has been completed.

Wedding Application Form

Wedding Information*

* This portion of the form is to be completed following your meeting with the minister.

Wedding Date _____ Time _____ Place _____

Rehearsal Date _____ Time _____ Place _____

Bride _____ Church Member? _____ Res. Phone _____

Bride's Address _____ Bus. Phone _____

Groom _____ Church Member? _____ Res. Phone _____

Groom's Address _____ Bus. Phone _____

Address after Marriage_____

First Marriage: Bride? _____ Groom? _____

Minister to Perform Ceremony _____Florist _____

Photographer _____ Number of Attendants _____

Organist/Pianist _____ Soloist(s) _____

Items to be provided by the church: Candelabra? _____

Aisle Candelabra? _____ Kneeling bench? _____

Will there be a church reception? _____ Location? _____

Number of attendees? _____

We agree to comply with the rules and regulations for marriage in this church.

Bride's Signature _____

Groom's signature _____

Date _____

Wedding Fees**

*** This portion of the form is to be completed at your meeting with the wedding coordinator.*

	Fee Amount	**Employee(s) to be paid**
1. Church Facilities	_____	_____
2. Organist/Pianist	_____	_____
3. Coordinator	_____	_____
4. Asst. to Coordinator**	_____	_____
5. Sound Technicians	_____	_____
6. Chase Candles	_____	_____
7. Other	_____	_____
Total	_____	

***The assistant to the coordinator is responsible for equipment setup and breakdown.*

The minister's honorarium is to be paid directly to the minister.

Couples Commitment Form

We pledge to:

1. Seek genuinely to discover what it means for Christ to be at the center of our relationship.

2. Be open before God to evaluating our relationship and whether or not we should marry. At any time between now and the wedding date, if either of us feels that marriage is not right for us, we will postpone or cancel the wedding.

3. Make every attempt to be on time and attend all sessions of the preparation-for-marriage class.

4. Commit ourselves to individually completing all homework assignments for the sessions, as well as discussing the assignment responses with each other.

5. Commit to not engaging in premarital sex. (If already involved: commit to abstain from further engagement in premarital sex and ask God for forgiveness.)

6. Seek to plan a worshipful wedding ceremony that will honor God and reflect the sacredness of the vows we make.

7. Agree to abide by the wedding policies of the church as outlined in the wedding policies manual.

8. Seek to understand biblical principles for Christian marriage as it relates to our roles in marriage, submission and authority in marriage, and spiritual leadership in marriage.

9. Seek to promote harmony among family members as we plan our wedding and as we live together in all the years of our marriage.

10. Seek competent Christian marital counseling if we should encounter problems with which we cannot deal.

We joyfully enter into this covenant.

Groom _____

Bride _____

Date _____

Premarital Interview Guidelines

––––––– ❧ –––––––

The initial step in premarital counseling through the preparation-for-marriage classes in our church is a couple's completion of the following questionnaire. They are each asked to respond in writing to these questions. Their responses to these questions are usually evaluated as a part of the other evaluations that are components of our preparation-for-marriage classes. If, however, a couple lives out of town and cannot make the class sessions, they are asked to complete this premarital interview questionnaire and return it to the pastor on our staff who will be performing the wedding. The couple is also required to seek premarital counseling in the city in which they reside.

The Interview Questions

General Information

1. How long have you known each other?

2. How long have you been engaged?

3. Does your family approve of your choice of a mate? If not, what are their reservations?

4. Are you well acquainted with your potential mate's immediate family? Describe your relationship with them.

5. Do you dislike any of your intended's family? If so, why?

6. Name several reasons that led you to desire to marry your potential mate.

7. What would you say makes a good marriage?

8. List three strengths and three weaknesses in your potential mate.

9. List three strengths and three weaknesses in yourself.

10. Are there any areas of your life that you find difficult to discuss openly with your potential mate? If so, what are they?

11. What would you consider as grounds for divorce?

12. Is there anything that makes you jealous of your potential mate?

13. In your opinion, what should be the limitations to a physical relationship before marriage? Be specific.

14. As a couple, how do you see God using you to serve others?

Background, Expectations, and Goals

1. Has divorce occurred in your family? Is yes, to whom?

2. List what you feel are the positive qualities of your father.

3. List what you feel are the positive qualities of your mother.

4. List what you feel are the negative qualities of your father.

5. List what you feel are the negative qualities of your mother.

6. In what ways are you similar to your father?

7. In what ways are you similar to your mother?

8. How well do you and your father communicate?

9. How well do you and your mother communicate?

10. What was/is your father's goal for your life?

11. What was/is your mother's goal for your life?

12. Was/is your parents' marriage a happy one?

13. Was/is your parents' marriage a spiritually strong one?

14. Which of your parents contributes the most strength to their marriage?

15. How do you expect your marriage to differ from your parents' marriage?

16. How do you expect your marriage to be similar to your parents' marriage?

17. What are your goals or aims in life? Have you discussed these with your potential mate?

18. In the following areas, what are your current goals/expectations for your marriage relationship: Spiritual? Economic? Recreational?

19. What are your goals in these areas for ten years from now?

Family and Home

1. How did your parents handle problems between them?

2. What was your response to your parents' method of handling their problems? What is your plan for settling problems?

3. How much influence should in-laws have on your marriage?

4. How do you feel about having children?

5. How many children would you like to have?

6. What would you say makes a good parent?

7. How do you think children should be disciplined?

8. How do you feel about the husband being the head of the home?

9. How do you feel about the wife working outside the home?

10. Are there any secrets that you should ever keep from each other?

11. If your mate were to become permanently paralyzed a month after your wedding, would you be willing to care for him/her the rest of your life? How would you cope with this tragedy?

Social

1. What are two activities (recreational, social, etc.) that the two of you have in common?

2. Would you be willing to permit your potential mate one night per week to pursue his/her own interests?

3. How important are special dates (anniversary, birthday, etc.) to you?

4. Do you dislike any of your potential mate's friends? If so, why?

5. Do the two of you have mutual friends? If so, how often do you socialize together?

6. What educational level have you and your potential mate attained? Does either of you plan on continuing your education? How do you feel about this?

Spiritual

1. Do you have a personal relationship with God through your responding in faith to the offer of salvation through Jesus Christ? At what age did you truly profess Jesus to be your Savior and Lord?

2. Are your parents Christians?

3. What is the greatest thing God has ever done for you?

4. What evidence is there in your life that you are a true believer in Christ?

5. Are you certain that your potential mate is a Christian? What evidence is there in his/her life that he/she is a true believer in Christ?

6. What would you like to see God do in and through your marriage?

7. Are you and your potential mate comfortable praying with each other? Are you comfortable studying God's Word together?

8. What church do you attend? What church does your potential mate attend? Do you two plan on worshiping at the same church? If not, why?

9. If you have children, do you and your potential mate agree on raising children in the family of faith? Do you both desire to worship with your children as a family at the same church?

Finances

1. Have you and your potential mate agreed on the income necessary to operate your household?

2. What do you feel is the scriptural approach to giving back a portion of your resources to the Lord?

3. Which of you is going to handle the money and the payment of bills?

4. What is your opinion of buying on credit?

5. Should you or your mate be allowed to have money for personal expenses? For what items?

6. Have you planned any kind of budget? Will? Insurance program?

Sex

1. What books have you read or to what tapes have you listened on the subject of sex in marriage?

2. Do you think your knowledge of physical and sexual relations is fair, good, or very good?

3. On a scale of 1 to 10, with 1 being the least important and 10 being the most important, how would you rate the importance of sex in marriage?

4. Does your potential mate know of any and all sexual experiences you may have had in the past?

5. Do you think your potential mate has a proper biblical understanding and awareness of his/her sexuality and is ready for marriage? Why?

6. Do you think you have a proper biblical understanding and awareness of your sexuality and are ready for marriage? Why?

7. Does the discussion of sexual matters with your potential mate make you embarrassed or inhibited?

Information Form for the Wedding Coordinator

———— ✤ ————

Bride _____ Home phone _____ Work phone _____

Groom _____ Home phone _____ Work phone _____

Wedding date _____ Time _____ Location _____

Rehearsal date _____ Time _____ Location _____

Minister _____ Home phone _____ Work phone _____

Names of Organist/Pianist _____

Names of Other Instrumentalists and the instrument played _____

_____

Names of Vocalists _____

Names of Maid/Matron of Honor, followed by the names of Bridesmaids _____

_____

_____

_____

Name of Best Man, followed by the names of Groomsmen _____

_____

_____

_____

Name of Flower Girl _____ Name of Ring Bearer _____

Names of two Groomsmen who will light candles _____

1. Please give some thought to the way you wish your attendants to enter the church and how you would like them to stand at the altar.

2. It might be helpful to attend a wedding at the church and observe how everything is done. You may arrange to do so by calling the church and securing the dates and times of weddings prior to yours.

3. Please list below (or on the back of this form) the names of parents, grandparents, and which groomsmen are to seat them in the ceremony. Please inform the wedding coordinator if there are divorced parents or grandparents who will be present, as this will help in planning where to seat these family members. Also, list any remarriages and if spouses will be present.

Bride's Family   Groom's Family

_____   _____

_____   _____

_____   _____

_____   _____

_____   _____

How many pews should be reserved for family members? _____

It is important that the wedding coordinator know the number and names of the songs you desire to use in the ceremony, as well as the names of the instrumentalists and vocalists performing the songs. Please make a copy of the completed "Wedding Music Form" and attach that to this form.

Please read carefully your wedding handbook. The answers to most questions can be found in this handbook. For other information, call your wedding coordinator.

Instrumental, Vocal, and Congregational Wedding Music

———— ❧ ————

Organ (or Piano) Selections for the Prelude*

Adagio/Sonata #1 in F Minor	Mendelssohn	Medium to Difficult
Aria (Be Thou with Them)	Bach	Medium Difficulty
Aria in F	Handel	Medium Difficulty
Arioso in A	Bach	Medium Difficulty
Claire de la Lune	Debussey	Medium Difficulty
Hymn by Vangelis	Arr. Irwin	Easy Difficulty
I Stand at the Threshold (*Sinfonia to Cantata #156 or Arioso*)	Bach	Medium Difficulty
Largo	Handel	Medium Difficulty
Nocturne	Chopin	Medium Difficulty
Paean	Chuckerbutty	Medium Difficulty

Sheep May Safely Graze	Bach	Medium to Difficult

Organ (or Piano) Selections for the Prelude or Seating of the Mothers*

Air for G String	Bach	Difficult
Ave Maria	Bach-Gounod	Medium Difficulty
Gabriel's Oboe	Marconne	Medium Difficulty
Jesu, Joy of Man's Desiring	Bach	Medium Difficulty
Liebestraum	Liszt	Difficult
Meditation on "Beecher" *(Love Divine, All Loves Excelling)*	Wilson	Medium Difficulty
Meditation from "Thais"	Massanet, arr. Joyce	Medium Difficulty
My Tribute	Crouch	Medium Difficulty
Pierre a Notre-Dame	Boellemann	Medium Difficulty
The Lord's My Shepherd	Simone	Medium Difficulty
The Swan	Saint-Saens	Medium Difficulty
Träumerei	Schumann	Medium Difficulty
Wedding Day *(O Perfect Love)*	Titcomb	Medium Difficulty

Organ (or Piano) Selections for the Prelude or Processional*

Canon in D	Pacabel	Medium Difficulty

Organ (or Piano) Selections for the Processional*

Bridal Chorus fr. Lohegrin	Wagner	Easy to Medium

Trumpet Voluntary in D Major	Clarke	Medium Difficulty
Wedding Processional *fr. "The Sound of Music"*	Rodgers	Easy to Medium

Organ (or Piano) Selections for the Processional or Recessional*

All Hail the Power *of Jesus' Name*	Jordan	Medium Difficulty
Festival Prelude on *"Coronation"* *(All Hail the Power of Jesus' Name)*	Martin	Medium Difficulty
Festival Trumpet Tune	Graham	Medium Difficulty
God of Grace and God of Glory	Mann	Medium Difficulty
Processional in G Major	Stanley	Medium Difficulty
Temple March	Kern	Medium Difficulty
Trumpet Tune in D Major	Clarke	Medium Difficulty

Organ (or Piano) Selections for the Prelude, Processional, Recessional, or Postlude*

Psalm XIX	Marcello	Medium Difficulty
Psalm XX	Marcello	Medium Difficulty
Rigaudon	Campra	Medium Difficulty
Trumpet Tune in D Major	Johnson	Medium Difficulty
Trumpet Tune in D Major	Purcell	Medium Difficulty

Organ (or Piano) Selections for the Prelude or Postlude*

Prelude in Classic Style	Young	Medium Difficulty

Organ (or Piano) Selections for the Recessional*

Four Seasons: Spring	Vivaldi	Medium Difficulty
Ode to Joy	Beethoven	Medium Difficulty
Wedding March from "A Midsummer Night's Dream"	Mendelssohn	Easy Difficulty

Organ (or Piano) Selections for the Recessional or Postlude*

Allergro Maestoso fr. "Water Music"	Handel	Medium to Difficult
Postlude fr. "Celebrate Life!"	Red	Medium Difficulty
Tocatta	Widor	Difficult

* Many of these are available in simplified versions.

Organ Collections: Easy Difficulty

Easy Wedding Music: Number One	arr. Perry	Lorenz Music
Easy Wedding Music: Number Two	arr. Wells	Lorenz Music
Our Wedding	arr. Wells	Lorenz Music

Organ Collections: Easy to Medium Difficulty

Something Old, Something New: Wedding Music for the Organ	arr. Martin	Lorenz Music
Standard Wedding Music	arr. Unknown	Lorenz Music
The Classical Organist	arr. Parks	Lillenas Music

Organ Collections: Medium Difficulty

The Complete Classical Wedding Book for Organ	arr. Barnard	Unity/Lorenz
The Diane Bish Wedding Book	arr. Bish	Gentry Music
Wedding Music: Book I	arr. Johnson	Augsburg
Wedding Music: Book II	arr. Johnson	Augsburg
Wedding Music for Organ	arr. Unknown	G. Schirmer

Organ Collections: Medium to Difficult

Wedding Music: Part I	arr. Unknown	Concordia
Wedding Music: Part II	arr. Unknown	Concordia

Piano Collections: Easy Difficulty

Chapel Voluntaries Book Nine: Wedding Music for Organ, Harmonium, or Piano	arr. Alphenaar	Edward B. Marks/ dist. Belwin Mills

Piano Collections: Easy to Medium Difficulty

Classical Transcriptions for Piano	arr. Smith	Lorenz Music

Piano Collections: Medium Difficulty

Church Piano Music	arr. Setchell	R. D. Row Music
Savior, Like a Shepherd Lead Us	arr. Whitworth	Broadman Music

Piano Collections: Medium to Difficult

Hymns with a Classical Touch	arr. Berry	Lillenas Music
Classical Praise Piano	arr. Keene	Maranatha Music

Vocal and Congregational Selections

Alleluia	Sinclair
Be Thou My Vision	Traditional
Because	Hardelot
Bless His Holy Name	Crouch
Bless the Lord, O My Soul	Traditional
Cherish the Treasure	Mohr
Entreat Me Not to Leave Thee (The Song of Ruth)	Gounod
Eternal Life	Dungan
Faithful Friend	Paris/Chapman
Find Us Faithful	Mohr
Flesh of My Flesh	Patillo
From All That Dwell Below the Skie	Hatton
Give Thanks	Smith
God, A Woman, and a Man	Green
Grace to You	Blakenship
Great Is the Lord	Smith
Great Is Thy Faithfulness	Runyan
Have Thine Own Way, Lord	Stebbins

Holy Ground	Davis
Holy, Holy	Owens
Holy Is the Lord	Schubert
Household of Faith	Lamb/Rosasco
How Beautiful	Paris
How Majestic Is Your Name	Smith
I Could Sing of Your Love Forever	Smith
I Give All My Life to You	Harris
I Love Thee	Grieg
I Love You, Lord	Klein
I Love You Truly	Jacobs-Bond
I Stand in Awe of You	Altrogge
I Will Be Here	Chapman
I'll Walk with God	Brodzky
In His Presence	Tunney
In My Life, Lord	Kilpatrick
In This Quiet Hour with God	Clark
In This Very Room	Harris
It Must Be Love	Mason
Jesus in Your Eyes	Miller
Joyful, Joyful, We Adore Thee	Beethoven
Lord, I Lift Your Name on High	Found
Lord's Prayer	Forsyth

Love Divine, All Loves Excelling	Zundel
Love Is the More Excellent Way	Mason
Make Us One	Johnson
May the Road Rise to Meet You	Turner
More Love to Thee	Doane
Morning Has Broken	Traditional
My Shepherd Will Supply My Need	Traditional
O Perfect Love	Barnby
O Promise Me	DeKoven
O Worship the King	Hadyn
Only God Could Love You More	Borop & Liles
Our Love	Scott, Coomer, North
Panis Angelicus (O Lord Most Holy)	Franck
Praise God, from Whom All Blessings Flow (The Doxolgy)	Bourgeois
Praise the Lord! Ye Heavens Adore Him	Prichard
Praise to the Lord, the Almighty	Traditional
Praise We Sing to Thee	Hadyn
Savior, Like a Shepherd Lead Us	Bradbury
Sheep May Safely Graze	Bach
Shine, Jesus, Shine	Kendrick
Shout to the Lord	McPherson
Shout to the Lord	Zschech

Surely the Presence of the Lord	Wolfe
Sweet, Sweet Spirit	Akers
Take My Life	Underwood
Take My Life, and Let It Be Consecrated	Malan
Take My Life, Lead Me, Lord	Rawls
That's the Way	Terry
The Bond of Love	Skillings
The Greatest of These Is Love	Carter
The Lord Bless You and Keep You	Lutkin
The Lord's Prayer	Malotte
The Majesty and Glory of Your Name	Fettke
The Parent's Prayer	Chapman
There Is None Like You	LeBlanc
Things I Cannot Say	O'Donnell
Time for Joy	Limpic
Together	Strader
We Exalt Thee	Sanchez, Jr.
We Will Glorify	Paris
Wedding Prayer	Dunlop
Wedding Song (There Is Love)	Traditional
What a Difference You've Made in My Life	Jordan
Wonderful Love	Kendrick
You Are My All in All	Proctor
You Are the Light	Fettke

APPENDIX G

Wedding Music Form

Bride _____ Home phone _____ Work phone _____

Groom _____ Home phone _____ Work phone _____

Wedding date _____ Time _____ Location _____

Minister _____ Home phone _____ Work phone _____

Coordinator _____ Home phone _____ Work phone _____

MUSICIANS

Organist _____ Home phone _____ Work phone _____

Pianist _____ Home phone _____ Work phone _____

Vocalist(s) _____ Home phone _____ Work phone _____

Instrumentalist(s) _____ Home phone _____ Work phone _____

MUSIC SELECTIONS
(Please submit a copy of all vocal music with this form.)

Prelude _____

Processional (Wedding Party) _____

   (Bride) _____

During ceremony _____

Recessional _____

Postlude _____

Approved _____ Date _____ Not Approved _____ Date _____

Please make a photocopy of this form to give to your wedding coordinator.

Scripture Index

---- ❧ ----

215

48:15–16   Ceremony 3
49:28   Ceremony 3

Numbers
6:24   Ceremony 2
6:24–26   Ceremony 3

Deuteronomy
6:1–2, 4–7   Ceremony 5
33:26   Ceremony 5
33:27   Ceremony 3

Joshua
1:5   Ceremony 14
23:14   Ceremony 15

Ruth
1:16–17   Ceremony 12

1 Samuel
18:3–4   Ceremony 4

Nehemiah
9:5   Ceremony 3

Psalms
27:1   Ceremony 3
31:12, 14–15   Ceremony 8
37:25–26, 28   Ceremony 5
51:10   Ceremony 10
51:17   Ceremony 8
57:8–9   Ceremony 5
71:23   Ceremony 5
84:5   Ceremony 3
100:4–5   Ceremony 16
113:1–4   Ceremony 3

Hebrews
4:16   Ceremony 8
10:10   Ceremony 6

James
1:17   Ceremonies 6, 11

1 Peter
3:7   Ceremony 20

2 Peter
3:9   Ceremony 15

1 John
3:1   Ceremony 1
3:16   Ceremony 1
3:18   Ceremony 1
4:7   Ceremony 17
4:7, 16   Ceremony 1
4:16   Ceremony 1
4:19   Ceremony 9

Revelation
19:6–9   Ceremony 5

Notes

Acknowledgments

1. S. I. Hayakawa, ed., *Reader's Digest Use the Right Word: A Modern Guide to Synonyms* (Pleasantville, N.Y.: Funk and Wagnalls, 1968), i–ii.

Chapter 3

1. *Uniquely You in Christ* Resources, Christian Impact Ministries, P.O. Box 490, Blue Ridge, Ga., 30513; 1-800-501-0490.

2. *Prepare/Enrich,* P.O. Box 190, Minneapolis, Minn., 55440-0190; 1-800-331-1661.

3. These companies may be contacted through the addresses or phone numbers provided above. Training usually involves a one-day commitment with the particular provider.

4. Five or more needed growth areas indicates a 93 percent chance of potential marital problems.

5. This material is not presently available for distribution.

Chapter 5

1. A vow is vertical in direction, as it is a solemn promise made by a person to God. An oath, more horizontal in direction, is an abbreviated covenant between two or more people with the name of God invoked as witness and guarantor. The vow normally includes an oath formula. In the Hebrew Bible, the wedding vow is actually an oath. It is referred to as a covenant only once, in Malachi 2:14.

Ceremony 1

1. Danny R. Smith, "A Wedding Celebration," *Proclaim* (spring 1994), 45.

2. Tim Grosshans, Executive Pastor, First Baptist Church, Orlando, Florida.

3. Leland Ryken, James C. Wilhoit, and Tremper Longman III, eds., "Honor," *Dictionary of Biblical Imagery* (Downer's Grove, Ill.: InterVarsity Press, 1998), 397.

4. Ibid., 399.

Ceremony 2

1. Author unknown, *Family Life* (January/February 1998), 24.

2. Mike Mason, *The Mystery of Marriage* (Portland, Ore.: Multnomah Press, 1985), 30.

Ceremony 3

1. Nehemiah 9:5.

2. 1 Timothy 6:15.

3. Romans 4:8.

4. Psalm 27:1.

5. Psalm 84:5.

6. Deuteronomy 33:27.

7. Isaiah 9:6.

8. Proverbs 3:33.

Ceremony 4

1. Kay Arthur, *Precepts from God's Word,* n.d.

2. Malachi 2:14.

Ceremony 7

1. George W. Thrush, Jr., "Wedding: Including Children from a Previous Marriage," *Proclaim* (October 1996), 42.

Ceremony 10

1. G. H. Palmer, "This Is the Hand," *HomeLife* (Nashville: Baptist Sunday School Board, August 1983).

Ceremony 11

1. Leland Ryken, James C. Wilhoit, and Tremper Longman III, eds., "Marriage," *Dictionary of Biblical Imagery* (Downer's Grove, Ill.: InterVarsity Press, 1998), 537–538.

Ceremony 12

1. C. Welton Gaddy, sermon entitled "Marriage—Myth or Miracle?" (Fort Worth, Tex.: Broadway Baptist Church, 1 October 1978).

2. Otis and Diegie Andrews, *Husbands and Wives, the Best Friends* (Nashville: Lifeway Press, 1994), 14.

3. Ibid., 22–23, 70.

4. Ibid., 108.

Ceremony 13

1. Gary Smalley, *Making Love Last Forever* (Dallas, Tex.: Word, 1996), 265.

2. Cyril J. Barber, *You Can Have a Happy Marriage* (Nashville: Thomas Nelson, 1984), 61.

Ceremony 14

1. O. S. Hawkins, *Tearing Down the Walls and Building Bridges* (Nashville: Thomas Nelson, 1995), 27.

Ceremony 15

1. Lewis B. Smeads, "The Power of Promising," *Christianity Today*, 21 January 1983, 16–19.

2. Cyril J. Barber, *You Can Have a Happy Home* (Nashville: Thomas Nelson, 1984), 47.

Ceremony 16

1. Mike Mason, *The Mystery of Marriage* (Portland, Ore.: Multnomah Press, 1985), 91.

2. Stuart Briscoe, "What Are Real Marriages Made Of?" *Preaching Magazine* (January/February 1990), 18–19.

3. Stanley Wiersma, "A Wedding Villanelle," *Christianity Today*, 7 November 1986, 69.

Ceremony 17

1. Mike Mason, *The Mystery of Marriage* (Portland, Ore.: Multnomah Press, 1985), 91.

2. John Maxwell Newsletter.

3. Mason, 97–98.

Ceremony 18

1. Howard J. Sala, *They Shall Be One Flesh* (Denver, Colo.: n.p., 1978), 109–110.

2. Ed Young, *Romancing the Home* (Nashville: Broadman Press, 1993), 117.

3. Jack R. Taylor, *What Every Husband Should Know* (Nashville: Broadman Press, 1981), 116.

4. David W. Augsburger, *Cherishable: Love and Marriage* (Scottdale, Pa.: Herald Press, 1971), 49.

5. Jack R. Taylor, *Husband*, 114.

6. Allan Peterson, ed., *Family Concern* (Omaha, Neb.: n.p., n.d.).

Ceremony 19

1. James C. Dobson, *Love for a Lifetime* (Portland, Ore.: Multnomah Press, 1987), 27.

2. Ibid., 20.

3. Richard Halverson, *Perspective*, 17 July 1991.

4. Ray C. Stedman, *Understanding Man* (Portland, Ore.: Multnomah Press, 1975), 37–38.

5. Mary Hayter, *The New Eve in Christ* (London: Wm. B. Eerdmans, 1987), 102.

6. H. C. Leupold, *Exposition on Genesis* (Ann Arbor, Mich.: Wartburg Press, 1942), 135.

7. Tim Timmons, *Maximum Marriage* (Old Tappan, N.J.: Fleming H. Revell, 1976), 33.

8. Gene A. Getz, *The Measure of a Marriage* (Ventura, Cal.: Regal, 1980), 17–18.

Ceremony 20

1. Gordan MacDonald, *Magnified Marriage* (Wheaton, Ill.: Tyndale House, 1983), 9.

2. John Maxwell, "What Does a Marriage Look Like?" *Growing Today* (San Diego, Cal.: Injoy, January 1997), 1.

3. John Drescher, "The Wedlock of Minds," *Christianity Today,* 6 June 1969, 127–128.

4. Author unknown, "The Covenant of Marriage," *Real Family Life* (Little Rock, Ark.: January/February 1998), 26.

5. Patricia A. Walton, "Hands," *The Lutheran Digest* (summer 1992), 72.

Appendices

Appendices A, B, C, D, E, G have been prepared by the staff of First Baptist Church/Orlando for use at the church.